Penguin Modern Poets

VOLUME 3

Glyn Maxwell was born in 1962 in Welwyn Garden City, Hertfordshire, of Welsh parents. He attended the universities of Oxford and Boston, where he studied poetry and playwriting under Derek Walcott. Three volumes of poetry, a book of plays and a novel have won him several awards. He divides his time between travelling abroad, writing at his home in West London and staging productions of his plays in the garden every two summers with his family.

Mick Imlah was born in Aberdeen and brought up near Glasgow. He was educated at Dulwich College and at Magdalen College, Oxford, where he was subsequently Junior Lecturer in English. He edited *Poetry Review* from 1983 to 1986, was Poetry Editor at Chatto & Windus publishing house from 1989 to 1993, and is now on the staff of *The Times Literary Supplement*. His poetry publications are *The Zoologist's Bath* and *Birthmarks*.

Peter Reading was born in Liverpool in 1946 and studied Fine Art at Liverpool College of Art, where, after a short spell as a schoolteacher, he returned to lecture in History of Art. In 1970 he moved to Shropshire, where he still lives and writes full time. Since the publication of his first collection of poems, *Water and Waste*, he has written many volumes of poetry, including *Nothing for Anyone*, *Fiction*, *Tom o' Bedlam's Beauties*, *Diplopic*, *Ukulele Music*, *Final Demands* and *Last Poems*. His two-volume *Collected Poems* will be published by Bloodaxe Books in 1995 and 1996. His poetry has been widely acclaimed, and he has been the recipient of the Cholmondeley Award, the Dylan Thomas Award and the Whitbread Award for Poetry. Peter Reading was elected a Fellow of the Royal Society of Literature in 1988.

Penguin Modern Poets

VOLUME 3

GLYN MAXWELL

MICK IMLAH

PETER READING

PENGUIN BOOKS

Published by the Penguin Group
Penguin Books Ltd, 27 Wrights Lane, London w8 5TZ, England
Penguin Books USA Inc., 375 Hudson Street, New York, New York 10014, USA
Penguin Books Australia Ltd, Ringwood, Victoria, Australia
Penguin Books Canada Ltd, 10 Alcorn Avenue, Toronto, Ontario, Canada M4V 3B2
Penguin Books (NZ) Ltd, 182–190 Wairau Road, Auckland 10, New Zealand

Penguin Books Ltd, Registered Offices: Harmondsworth, Middlesex, England

This selection first published 1995
10 9 8 7 6 5 4 3 2 1

Typeset by Datix International Limited, Bungay, Suffolk
Printed in England by Clays Ltd, St Ives plc
Set in 10.5/13pt Monophoto Garamond

Contents

vi

Glyn Maxwell

Peter Brook

Let every page
Begin as clean
And end as clear
As stories are
If actors pass
Through pain and grace
To make a stage
Of any place.

Let every word
Be prized enough
Shyly to talk
Or weep with work
Or fail afresh
Towards a truth
That may be heard
Beyond its breath.

Let every gap
And every strip
Of space fulfil
Its hapless will
That all about
Each uttered mark
The matter drop
Into the dark.

Let every line
In ignorance
Of whence it came
Or what's to come
Hold out its hands
Into the breeze
As I do mine
And cling to these.

Rare Chat with the Red Squirrel

No even now, when your
once astonished, once muttering, once
blurting, lastly listening faces group
and grey in a demi-circle in this home garden,
I can surprise you.

Not with my rare colour,
– you protest at 'rare', you who had, yes you,
pinned me down on your recto 'Extinct in England',
and you who scribbled 'hoax' when you even saw me,
manning the riddled elm,

or after, at my capture,
sniffed round me like a wine-sharp, or a
buyer about to nudge his honey and show her
'you see this is painted on' – but even then
you wouldn't have it:

you merely substituted
'common' then, like it made you less the wrongdoer,
envisaging squads of us and I the ringleader
swiftly nailed. You wouldn't believe a murmur
on my bushy red honour.

Nor when the grey,
fresh from his walnut elevenses,
bared his teeth at the bars till the cops inferred
yes, I was that victim and made me feel so
strangely guilty

as he was handled away,
and I said, 'You dig, that wasn't the actual grey
who did my nutkin over – he was another,
and I'd know his red eyes anywhere, 'cause
hell, I'm in them,' no,

you caged me again,
and locked and stood and pondered what I did.
It was sodding dark in there with my surname's red
uncaught by light, so nothing. I cocked my head
for one measly eureka

but the way it went was, like,
a burning bath to see if my red would leak,
an X-ray into what was making me talk,
a bastard prod to see what made me not talk,
a mugshot, an APB –

fine, fine way to love me.
But gentlemen, ladies, that is the better-left-
unsaid past you notice I always say.
You would too, but let us enjoy this day.
Everybody looks grey

who waits in the oaks
and ashes for that time when with my eyes
hurt on a text, and nuts beside my nut-tray,
Nature takes her run up and I'm quick with love
but not quick enough, so,

in the long mean time,
listen only to how the noise you hear
in your wide language differs in no respect
from what you heard when I first happened on nut,
or burst from the grey horde

who got the rest, for I know
you listen to me not for a new wisdom,
nor music nor aloneness in my England,
and nor for what remains of my red coat,
nor that you thought me dead,

though that perturbed you
maybe a little, no? You know it's only
my bound, hic and squeak when I rub my eyes.
Beats me why, cross my heart, but it's a song
you should recognize.

Farm Close

The small field by my house is the small field
I mean: the old green field of incidents,
small teams, comments and the planned insult.

It's just the same to look at, like my book
with the Straw-Witch on page 9, the frightener!
It doesn't frighten me, but nothing does.

On the small field now, different goalkeepers
minding their own when the quarrel starts
and different bullies asking, but still doomed

to weeks in jail or profits in South London.
Different targets too, but they deserve it,
and I feel towards them like the ones we had.

Just drab men punching in the rain.
For me to stop them, stop the usual hurt,
would be to disrupt the business of a town,

or change the future of a small, determined planet.
And I'm just the mad beloved Time-Traveller
who, as you probably know, can't do that.

Dream but a Door

Dream but a door slams then.
Your waking is in the past. The friend
who left was the last to leave and that
left you, calm as a man.

Wash in a slip of soap belonging
only a week ago to a girl but
yours now and washed to a nothing.
As you and she, friends and not.

Eat to the end as toast,
the loaf she decided on, only last
Saturday last. The crust is what
you said you'd have. So have.

Stop by the calendar, though,
and peel. The colour today
is yellow, and you will never remember
what that means – 'J'.

Drink to the deep the coffee, down
to the well of the dark blue cup.
The oaf with the nose of steam is alive
and well again. Look up.

EC3

Her heart alert and in on things she walks
quickeningly by my side. Her looks
are mirrored dustily on glass that mirrors
crane and ruin high over her. She *is*
    the Eyecatcher. This *is*
    the real City. Some terrors

for me are terrors for her but look how the dust
of drilled churches skips her with a gust
that blinds old me. I blink into all men
dressed as what they are and were all day
    and were all yesterday
    passing neglecting on, un-

der irredeemable heights of rocking steel.
I'd scurry from so high, or seem to kneel
from gap to remaining gap towards remains.
She guides by this, blonde of a village past,
    glancing noticed past.
    My interested remains

hurry on beside what eyes still go
up, down, up, down hopefully and no,
through one bulb-lit and tiny violet cave,
then out between the vital youngster drunk
    and useless ruin drunk,
    where leaden, beaten love

does with what it has. This *is* the mile
ahead. Abandon stabs at it. These pale
scuttling creatures under the high nod
of the pudgy near-to-dead are in it now.
　　We thread on by it now,
　　exchange the affecting nod,

and pass below, away to our ticking homes.
No nothing in the tallest of my dreams
'll grow as tall as, falling up and down
as that, or hook these red uncrediting eyes
　　like the Eyecatcher's eyes
　　in the dead east of town.

Song to the Skinhead

'Ginger, you are going to die.'
I am, but was that what you meant,
that summer night you cycled by
while I was on my steady way
home and watched you pedal away
        not watching where I went?

I haven't yet. What did you mean?
You haven't either. Yes, I'd know
– I'd even care – but I haven't seen
your mugshot on a local page
with how or when you went, your age,
        or where the wreaths should go.

We're older now. You haven't said
a word since 'You are going to die'
(to me, I mean) and well, we've led
extremely different kinds of lives
since. I haven't carried knives.
        You probably don't sigh.

But well, I will say this. There are some
moments from the time they are
until the time we're not, that come
and never weaken, never fade,
and you created one that stayed
        and will, like any star:

'Ginger, you are going to die,'
you said, and biked into the blue.
For that, and that I haven't, I –
thank you. When I need to know
that any can be loved, I do
        tend to begin with you.

Exit Krull

From *The Birthday Ball of Zelda Nein*, Act I, Scene x

There will not be a Ball. It's just as well,
For I was never here. Perhaps you'll tell
That to the men who stand at your open door,
Taking out my photograph once more.
     Remember you never saw me.

I am not one of these nor one of you.
I vote for neither the scarlet nor the blue.
I have no information to impart,
Nor plot nor plan nor sabotage to start.
     Remember you never saw me.

I am the one you always fail to place,
The never blurred but never circled face,
The one no one remembers having known,
Who leaves no man alone but leaves alone.
     Remember you never saw me.

One will have been invited and left last.
Two will attempt too much and too fast.
Three will be standing cold on the third day.
And the uninvited blow this world away.
     Remember you never saw me.

CHORUS
We won't be treated like this. We're going then.
We may not come again.

Either

A northern hill aghast with weather
Scolds and lets me hurry over.
Someone phoned to tell my father
Someone died this morning of a
Stroke. The news has tapped me with a
Stick. I vaguely knew his brother.
No one knows where I am either.

Now I'm lost. I don't know whether
This road runs along the river
Far enough. I miss my lover,
Town and all the south. I'd rather
Die than be away forever,
What's the difference. Here's another
Field I don't remember either.

The Albatross Revolution

1

The Residence was coddled by the light
of albatrosses, many of them silent.

The summerhouse had had a green door then,
which banged and banged and shut, and the relevant

daughters of their Highnesses were to be seen
nowhere – probably putting on a play

or, at that flashpoint of the century,
heading somewhere new, reluctantly.

2

The albatrosses having flown inland,
the green door flew open. The daughters and

the friends they had were two groups that were not
there, and starlings were a small group that was,

though not for long. The lawn was wide and cold
with all these new commotions, and the sea

licked at the bony ankles of the cliff
as if it was their Highnesses. It rained.

3

Somebody laughed hysterically when
the full whiteness of the Residence

exposed itself to all – the random all
who shoved each other out of the forest now.

The starlings jabbed in the orangery.
The albatrosses did something different

elsewhere, the details quite available.
There was some sour cream in the Residence.

4

There were some bottles in the sea. The cliff
had stood ten centuries of them, and would,

to be honest, stand twenty centuries more.
Men climbed the chimneys of the Residence

even as podgy womenfolk exchanged
recipes involving cheese and sour cream.

And they flew flags, the men. And starling crap
made constellations on the cold wide lawn.

5

It rained. Whatever the flag meant, it sulked
or, at that flashpoint of the afternoon,

resulted in all sorts of things. The cream
was put to its sour use. The Residence

was multi-purpose, snaps of albatrosses
hung all about. The air grew dark and green

as uniforms, and, catapulting out
of a high window, the Albatross-Man.

Sport Story of a Winner

He was a great ambassador for the game.
       He had a simple name.
His name was known in households other than ours.
       But we knew other stars.
We could recall as many finalists
       as many panellists.
But when they said this was his Waterloo,
       we said it was ours too.

His native village claimed him as its own,
       as did his native town,
adopted city and preferred retreat.
       So did our own street.
When his brave back was up against the wall,
       our televisions all
got us shouting and that did the trick.
       Pretty damned quick.

His colours were his secret, and his warm-up
       raindance, and his time up
Flagfell in the Hook District, and his diet
       of herbal ice, and his quiet
day-to-day existence, and his training,
       and never once explaining
his secret was his secret too, and his book,
       and what on earth he took

that meant-to-be-magic night in mid-November.
　　　　You must remember.
His game crumbled, he saw something somewhere.
　　　　He pointed over there.
The referees soothed him, had to hold things up.
　　　　The ribbons on the Cup
were all his colour, but the Romanoff
　　　　sadly tugged them off.

We saw it coming, didn't we. We knew
　　　　something he didn't know.
It wasn't the first time a lad was shown
　　　　basically bone.
Another one will come, and he'll do better.
　　　　I see him now – he'll set a
never-to-be-beaten time that'll last forever!
　　　　Won't he. Trevor.

The Eater

Top of the morning, Dogfood Family!
How's the chicken? How's the chicken?
Haven't you grown? Or have you grown,
here in the average kitchen at noontime
      down in the home, at all?

Bang outside, the bank officials
are conga-dancing and in their pinstripe
this is the life! But it isn't your life
out in the swarming city at crushhour
      dodging humans, is it?

Vacant city – where did they find that?
Blossom of litter as the only car
for a man goes by. When the man goes by
his girl will sulkily catch your eye:
      will you catch hers?

Snow-white shop – how do they do that?
Lamb-white medical knowing and gentle
man, advise her, assure and ask her:
do you desire the best for your children
      and theirs? Well *do you?*

Take that journey, delight in chocolate,
you won't find anyone else in the world,
lady, only the man, the sweet man
opening doors and suggesting later
      something – what thing?

Short time no see, Dogfood Family!
How's the chicken? How's the chicken?
How have you done it? Have you done it
with love, regardless of time and income
and me? Who am I?

I am the eater and I am the eater.
These are my seconds and these are my seconds.
Do you understand that? Do you get that,
you out there where the good things grow
and rot? Or not?

Wasp

We were all strained with the food when look, a wasp
was and saw what it smelt on our white table
that damnably good summer: it saw the best

thing for now. The bee was near but wiser,
off engineering better from her own
mauve flowers in a basket off the hot wall:

she didn't want what we had wanted and had,
our spoils and fluids. The wasp rose out and passed
from salad to salad, amazed, I suppose, with how many

there were to approach and envisage. You,
suddenly poised, with a weapon
lightly awaiting, waited. And when I looked

you all had coshes and swatters and so did I.
The nasty little guy
chose to buzz our heads and would die because

of what it wanted and was.
We enjoyed that animal pause in our long lunch,
armed, mates in sweat and our local luck.

We got it. Who got it? I got it,
and dissuaded the boys from keeping it
frizzing in a jar forever and ever. I crushed it.

Well, I thought, as the bee moved off to tell –
but heavily, bored with its maddening cousins – well:
don't fuck with us, little guys. We're mad as hell.

Car Game

His first he said was in HONOUR but not in GLORY.
He steered through the shattered village.
His second was not in SALT nor was it in PEPPER.
We were no wiser.
We passed a place-name slashed with a thick red line
To say that was it, gone, over.

His third, and we sucked our peppermints as he drove,
Was in both RHYME and RHYTHM.
We went by a farm and his fourth was not in FARM
But was in FERME.
'No?' he taunted, expecting us to be guessing
In his sickeningly warm

Old Citroën, and his fifth was not in SIGHT
But was in SPRIGHTLINESS
Of all things and we climbed a desolate hill.
I was unwell,
What with the churning and turning and him with his sixth
In JACK but not in JILL.

The tollbooth was abandoned, and we slid
The faces on our passes
Back inside our coats, then out again
To swap and grin.
His seventh was not in TIME or SPACE. Someone
Yawned 'What is it then?'

In vain of course. We could feel his smile. By now
We were out of the worst of it,
Unless it had spread this far. His last was in GOD
And CLOUD, he said.
His clue was 'We're for it now', so I said 'Homeland'
And watched his still grey head.

The Altered Slightly

Hilarious to the virus that has spent
its infinite resources
concocting itself anew,

these healers, helicoptered into a war zone,
with helmets and a peace plan,
pound the maps in a shell of an HQ.

Under the microscope the enemies goggle
in yellow and red grease,
their tricorn shapes a shock, and somebody says

*That's them but if you look
they've altered slightly.* Good news for the sniper,
who sights the Muslim wandering up the road,

then sights the Christian limping in the gutter,
and cannot choose between them or to let them
come and have each other. The dead,

uniquely in the dark about who did it,
lie still as stone, mistaken for the hiding,
while somewhere in some dedicated rich

lab the virgin germs,
nervous in molecular pitch dark,
parachute into a slide of blood

and set to work.

The Sarajevo Zoo

Men had used up their hands, men had
offered, cupped, or kissed them to survive,
had wiped them on the skirts of their own town,
as different men had shinned up a ladder and taken
    the sun down.

One man had upped his arms in a victory U
to a thousand others, to show how much of the past
he did not know and would not know when he died.
Another's joke was the last a hostage heard:
    Oh I lied

which did win some applause from the bare hands
of dozing men. And others of course had never
fired before, then fired, for the work of hands
was wild and sudden in those days
    in those lands.

For men. For the women there was
the stroke, the ripping of hair, the smearing of tears,
snot, and there was the prod of a shaking man,
or with fused palms the gibbering prayer
    to the UN.

The nothing they had between those palms was
hope and the yard between surrendering palms
was hope as well. Far off, a fist in the sky
was meaning hope but if you prised it open
    you saw why.

The hands of the children here were wringing themselves
hot with the plight of animals over there,
and drawing them in their pens with the crimson rain
of what men do to each other on television
         crayoned in.

But hands continued to feed the demented bear
who ate two other bears to become the last
bear in the Sarajevo Zoo. And they fed him
when they could, two Bosnian zookeepers
         all autumn.

Today I read that that time ended too,
when fifteen rifles occupying some thirty
hands got there and crept in a rank on knees
towards the smoke of the blown and stinking cages
         and black trees.

Trees were what you could not see the starving
beasts behind, or see there were now no beasts,
only the keepers crouching with their two lives.
Then winter howled a command and the sorry branches
         shed their leaves.

Springs of Simon Peter

In a town in which to have tried three times
he rose and he spent such afternoons
    between his friends
    at Jim's and Tom's
and out, having so chuckled of each
to the other he'd never be out of touch.

Days were for blame and invite; nights
were many though he could have had more, he reckoned,
    and every second
    was up in lights
but he tottered home and peered at his board
for messages and the word was LORD.

And then it was blank and always so,
a tabula rasa coloured lavender
    only. The calendar
    had less to show
as he riffled it forwards. Here came Jim
but he'd gone by then, when here came Tom.

The next fresh four a.m. he was treading
deazil around the Lake and the thought
    in his head was what
    he was clearly reading
on stones, dates and pages, an ache
to hear, register, shiver, and speak

to stranger and stranger, mentioned, shunned,
a punchline: he would wait in the dust
    all night for the first
    and freezing sound
of the barracking cock, and a surge of sudden
what? then home to his hissing garden

and huge, turning keys. In a town
in which to have tried three times he would lie
    as the very day
    would break, with his fawn
long arms hiding the falls of his face
from his own words spreading through the whole of
    space.

Thief on the Cross

How are you doing on yours, my pal
in crime? Are you off where the hurt has hurt so far
    it's what life is, and before
was all the goners like us will ever cop
    of *paradiso*? Well?

Or are you flapping away in the three
agonies, my apprentice? Is that what
    fixes your look on the flat
world we were caught and tried in, makes you turn
    lollingly from me?

Why ever it is – is it your lips?
dry as the lot will be by the squawking dawn,
    dusty as all by noon? –
you've barely cracked a word in our lingo since
    that tin-tiled cyclops

pegged us to our final form,
condemned by imperial thieves to peg as thieves,
    unmissed. Those wailing wives
are crawling back to the feet of our mate in front:
    that triples the hurt for him

in any case. I'm glad we two
purloined a moment's peace from the long pain
    it turned into. Not again --
you're going to ask him again, aren't you? Aren't you
    satisfied? I tell you,

feckless snivelling rascal whelp:
we're only smack bang where our blessed old dears
        predicted, all those years
gone: but this one isn't one of us lot.
        He's innocent, he can't help.

And Leaves Astonishing

For now, among the falling of the ochres,
Reds and yellows, in which haze the many
   Casualties of what on earth
Went on here this month, re-fuse, this joker's
Pockets open out and he digs for money.

His the face suggested to, spat on,
In which the door and final door were shut,
   The mother of which saw and lost
At stations, and the quizzes of the Western
Shows made to a shape you don't forget:

Human of the Revolution, soul
We would wouldn't we be if our dreams
   Loomed amateur cine of tanks
Slowing round our corner and the whole
Hope thing holed and fumbling in own homes –

For now he buys and smokes and his rivered mug
Grins above the inhalation. It all
   Rustles by beyond him now,
The elbowing to run the show, the lag
Of bloody onus, economic stall,

The eloquence and begging in the States
And books of what it was, means, portends.
   Photographed and asked, he moves
His hand to – what, to offer cigarettes
Nobody takes. He takes and lights one, stands

And leaves, astonishing the siding rich
With just being. The love sticks on the tongue.
   He goes his way, who went his way,
Where talk is meant and lit, at the throat's hutch,
On streets of blood, in cafés of the lung.

Helene and Heloise

So swim in the embassy pool in a tinkling breeze
The sisters, *mes cousines*, they are blonde-haired
   Helene and Heloise,
One for the fifth time up to the diving board,
The other, in her quiet shut-eye sidestroke
Slowly away from me though I sip and look.

From in the palace of shades, inscrutable, cool,
I watch exactly what I want to watch
   From by this swimming pool,
Helene's shimmer and moss of a costume, each
Soaking pony-tailing of the dark
And light mane of the littler one as they walk;

And the splash that bottles my whole life to today,
The spray fanning to dry on the porous sides,
   What these breathtakers say
In their, which is my, language but their words:
These are the shots the sun could fire and fires,
Is paid and drapes across the stretching years.

Now Heloise will dive, the delicate slimmer,
Calling Helene to turn, who turns to see
   One disappearing swimmer
Only and nods, leans languorously away
To prop on the sides before me and cup her wet
Face before me near where I'd pictured it.

I was about to say I barely know them. –
I turn away because and hear of course
   Her push away. I see them
In my rose grotto of thought, and it's not a guess,
How they are, out of the water, out
In the International School they lie about,

What they can buy in the town, or the only quarters
Blondes can be seen alighting in, and only
   As guided shaded daughters
Into an acre of golden shop. 'Lonely?'
Who told me this had told me: 'They have no lives.
They will be children. Then they will be wives.'

Helene shrieks and is sorry – I don't think – my
Ankles cool with the splash of her sister's dive:
   I wave and smile and sigh.
Thus the happiest falling man alive,
And twenty-five, and the wetness and the brown
Hairs of my shin can agree, and I settle down.

'Already the eldest – suddenly – the problems.
The other draws, writes things.' I had heard
   Staccato horrid tantrums
Between earshot and the doorbell, held and read
Heloise's letters in chancery
Script to her dead grandmother, to me,

To nobody. They have a mother and father,
And love the largest pandas in the whole
   World of Toys. The other
Sister rang from Italy and was well,
But wouldn't come this time. 'She'll never come.
She has a home. They do not have a home.'

Stretching out in her shiny gold from the pool,
Heloise swivels, and sits and kicks
      Then reaches back to towel
Her skinny shoulders tanned in a U of lux-
Uriant material. Helene
Goes slowly to the board, and hops again

Into the dazzle and splosh and the quiet. Say,
Two, three miles from here there are heaps of what,
      Living things, decay,
The blind and inoculated dead, and a squad
Of infuriated coldly eyeing sons
Kicking the screaming oath out of anyone's.

Cauchemar. We will be clear if of course apart,
To London again me, they to their next
      Exotic important spot,
Their chink and pace of Gloucestershire, Surrey, fixed
Into the jungles, ports or the petrol deserts.
I try but don't see another of these visits,

As I see Helene drying, Heloise dry,
The dark unavoidable servant seeming to have
      Some urgency today,
And my book blank in my hands. What I can love
I love encircled, trapped and I love free.
That happens to, and happens to be, me,

But this is something else. Outside the fence,
It could – it's the opposite – be a paradise
      Peopled with innocents,
Each endowed with a light inimitable voice,
Fruit abundant, guns like dragons and giants
Disbelieved, sheer tolerance a science –

Still, I'd think of Helene, of Heloise
Moving harmless, shieldless into a dull
     And dangerous hot breeze,
With nothing but hopes to please, delight, fulfil
Some male as desperate and as foul as this is,
Who'd not hurt them for all their limited kisses.

The Clearest Eyes

The clearest eyes in our dear hemisphere
Could make out that the x of army plane
That is an answer to what is a prayer
Took off last night in silence from Orion.

La Brea

Los Angeles. So just
guess what I saw: not the dust
or the wide jammed road, not that. And not
the park where enormous playthings eat

the shouting children. No, and the glass white
televised cathedral? – that
was a sight seen for the sin-
gle flashed moment, and gone.

I saw the tar-pits at La Brea,
where a dark endowed museum squats, and where
the thick blots of lake are watched,
and the haired replicas stroked and touched

by kiddies. There's a tour:
the intelligible stone, the Short-Faced Bear,
the Dire Wolf, American Lion and Mastodon,
and Man with not much brain.

Well they did all make a dumb
choice that day! But my day was warm
and fascinating. Try to see these
tar-pits, at La Brea, in Los Angeles.

My Turn

I have been so enchanted by the girls
who have a hunch, I have been seen

following them to the red and green
see-saws. There have been a few of them

I recognized. I have been recognized.
I have stood on the roundabout and turned.

I have swung, uselessly, not as high as them.
Then seen the parents coming, and the rain

On rusty and unmanned remaining things.
I have calculated west from the light cloud.

Cried myself dry and jumped
back on the roundabout when it had stopped.

Started it again, in the dark wet,
with my foot down, then both my feet on it.

Desire of the Blossom

This strain bloomed red. It became tended:
Admirable, colourful, a flower
In the good corner. No more green wildfire
Threatening no promising: that
    Pollen-coaxing
Act had ended.

And eyes had me, noses neared and dwindled.
Cameras' mutated insect heads.
Partakers came to tag all sorts of reds
They marked in me: Royal Mail Red,
    Robin and Blood Red,
Vigil Candle,

Ibis, Ripper, Cardinal and Crab-
Apple. Then they went and I remain
This pleased awhile, in a glow – sane,
Boiling with their help, cooled
    Fitfully by the night
And the dew-web

Nagging me woken, wired, sustained – red.
But say, of a morning, may I (dreamt I) one
Morning shake like an animal in rain
These ribbons off and look
    A neglected species
The colour Mud?

Cause if, I would remove to a far garden,
Cold, unphotogenic, dry to the sight,
Proffering no petal, no respite
From strict time, then ugly,
    Vegetable, fibrous,
Strain and harden.

State of the Nation

Now any word from you is a new word,
As gnarled and unawaited as the new
Could ever be, the tongue of the grim few
Who burnt my flag, and I did have a flag.
I had, like we all had, the shape of shroud
Or swaddling with me gone from it. That flag.

And any news of you is propaganda.
In that I can believe it well enough,
Or that it was concocted by your staff
To be believed. All but the oldest pictures
We mock as forgeries, and my children wonder
What I am always burning and I go *Witches*.

No, I have let them clean across my country,
The people of your land, in happier times,
I've neither known nor cared about their crimes,
But neither have I let them stay. I trust
They know the points of exit and of entry
Can still be told apart in the red dust.

And yes, I have corresponded with your greats,
Translated work, remembered stanzas, lines,
Partaken of your wisdom as your wines,
And told my countrymen: They are the Past,
But they had jokes and hopes and secret dates,
They thought their paste-and-paper homes would last,

And that their prayers were heard. – But it's the Law,
Or is it here. Your earth is blown and lost.
You work forever in a birdless west
In binary. You will not be received.
Your immigrants will be turned out at door.
Their fantasies and nothing else believed.

Your treasures we will lick into clean plates,
And wring the loaded clouds so very tight
They bulge apart and wash your picnics out,
We sorely hope. Our likeliest to die
Will dream you up when he hallucinates.
The best of us will cross and pass you by.

But don't assume we do this to our other
Neighbour, where they whistle the To-Come.
Her citizens are made to feel at home
As long as they require it. They belong.
All borders are the same, except the border
Between our kind and you. That's barbed and strung,

Uncrossable, too long for the pinched age
We have as nations. Say there's still some meadow
Where we could meet or send in place a shadow
To make the signs we would. That would be news.
Perhaps in your gone country there's a stage
For puppetry. It would at least amuse.

My motorcade went miles along the border
One April night. I listened and saw nothing.
Then there was distant rocketfire, then nothing,
A pitiless cold dark. It's said we're winning
(Admittedly by me, and it's an order)
But when the morning breaks I think we're winning,

The salmon light falls freshly on the schools
I built, and loyal students in the squares
Are gulping down espressos as I pass,
And every evening all the theatres shine
With characters we know and love, and tales
That never were, but happen, and are mine.

Just Like Us

It will have to be sunny. It can rain only
when the very plot turns on pain and postponement,
the occasional funeral. Otherwise perfect.

It will have to be happy, at least eventually
though never ending and never exactly.
Somebody must, at the long-last party,

veer to the side, to remember, to focus.
All will always rise to a crisis,
meet to be shot for a magazine Christmas.

It will also be moral: mischief will prosper
on Monday and Thursday and seem successful
but Friday's the truth, apology, whispered

love or secret or utter forgiveness.
It will have to be us, white and faulty,
going about what we go about. Its

dark minorities will *be* minorities,
tiny, noble and gentle, minor
characters in more offbeat stories.

Its favourite couple will appear in our towns,
giving and smiling. Their tune will be known
by all from the lonely to the very young

and whistled and sung. It will all be repeated
once. Its stars will rise and leave,
escaping children, not in love,

and gleam for a while on the walls of girls,
of sarcastic students beyond their joke,
of some old dreadful unhappy bloke.

It will have to be sunny, so these can marry,
so these can gossip and this forgive
and happily live, so if one should die

in this, the tear that lies in the credible
English eyes will be sweet, and smart
and be real as blood in the large blue heart

that beats as the credits rise, and the rain
falls to England. You will have to wait
for the sunny, the happy, the wed, the white. In

the mean time this, and the garden wet
for the real, who left, or can't forget,
or never meant, or never met.

Drive to the Seashore

We passed, free citizens, between the gloves
of dark and costly cities, and our eyes
bewildered us with factories. We talked.

Of what? Of the bright dead in the old days,
often of them. Of the great coal-towns, coked
to death with scruffy accents. Of the leaves

whirled to shit again. Of the strikers sacked
and picking out a turkey with their wives.
Of boys crawling downstairs: we talked of those

but did this: drove to where the violet waves
push from the dark, light up, lash out to seize
their opposites, and curse to no effect.

Poem in Blank Rhyme

This isn't very difficult to do.
The sky's pink, the morning pretty new.

Last night I met a mate from the old crew.
We walked too far too late and turned a U

Out of the woods as it got dark. He knew
I'd spend the evening talking about you

But didn't mind, and, when we had to queue,
He made the time fly quickly with his two

Dozen unfunny jokes, plus a big clue
About his own big heart. Well the sky's blue

Now over there, I'm standing in the dew,
Remembering and hoping. But it's true:

Days are very many. Days are few.
I want to be with someone and you're who.

Curse on a Child

'Darlin', think of me as a stoppin' train. I go all the way, but you can
get off anywhere you like.'

— Male advance, overheard

May the love of your life get on at Ongar
  And wake up sleeping on Terminal 4.
May his anorak grow big with jotters
  Noting the numbers of trains he saw.
May he read these out in a reedy voice,
  May he drink real ale with his mates while you
Blink in the smoke. May his hair be a joke.
  May his happiest hour have been spent in Crewe.

May he call for you in a lime-green van,
  May his innermost thoughts be anyone's guess.
May his answer to 'Who's your favourite band?'
  Be the only occasion he answers 'YES,'
But then may he add, 'When Wakeman was with 'em,'
  And play you the evidence. May what he wears
Never again be in vogue. May his mother
  Dote, devote, and move in downstairs.

May your French turn frog, may your croissant go
    straight,
  May your bread be Hovis, your wine home-made,
May your spice be Old Spice, your only lingerie
  Les fronts-igrec, and your beauty fade.
May you curl in the Land of Nod like the child
  You were when you wouldn't, and screamed all the way
From Perpignan to the Gare de Lyon,
  Echoed through Paris, and on to Calais.

The man in the corner, who sat with his head
    Awake in his hands, has issued this curse.
He is far away now. What keeps him awake
    Isn't screaming, crying, or writing verse.
It is sometimes nothing but quiet, sloping,
    My terrible infant, looming and deep.
May you never know it. May your life be as boring
    As men can make it, but, dear, may you sleep.

Rumpelstiltskin

'Your name is Rumpelstiltskin!' cried
The Queen. 'It's not,' he lied. 'I lied
The time you heard me say it was.'
'I never heard you. It's a guess,'

She lied. He lied: 'My name is Zed.'
She told the truth: 'You're turning red,
Zed.' He said: 'That's not my name!'
'You're turning red though, all the same.'

'Liar!' he cried, 'I'm turning blue.'
And this was absolutely true.
And then he tore himself in two,
As liars tend to have to do.

Plaint of the Elder Princes

We are the first and second sons of Kings.
We do the most incredibly stupid things.
   When we meet Elves
    We piss ourselves;
When we see adults walking around with wings,

We crack up laughing and we take the mick.
We wind up in a cloud or we get sick,
   Or turned to stone,
    Or wedding a crone
And running widdershins and damned quick,

Or otherwise engaged, up to our eyes.
We brag, we stir, we mock and we tell lies.
   Upon our Quest
    Eight Kingdoms west
We find no peace. Nobody evil dies.

No, seven Witches have a Ball and go to it.
Our sweethearts meet a toad and say hello to it.
   We bet it's our
    Brother De-ar:
It is, we ask a favour, he says no to it.

We are the first and second sons of Queens.
We have our chances and our crucial scenes
   But it comes up Tails
    While Our Kid scales
The castle walls with some wild strain of beans

To make his dream come out. What about ours?
We've wished on every one of the lucky stars,
   Got on with Wizards
    And off with Lizards,
Sung the gobbledegook to Arabian jars,

But no: we serve to do the right thing wrong,
Or do the bad thing first, or stagger along
    Until it's time
    For the Grand Old Rhyme
To drop and make our suffering its song.

The Fool implied that we were 'necessary'
In his last lay. This made us angry. Very.
    Perhaps we are
    But his guitar
Has found a lodging quite unsanitáry.

'Typical Them!' we hear them say at court:
'Brutal, selfish, arrogant, ill-taught!'
    They *thought* we would
    Turn out no good
And lo, we turned out just as they all thought,

We first and second Princes of the Blood.
Dreaming of a woman in a wood.
    Scaring the birds,
    Lost for words,
Weeds proliferating where we stood;

But hell, we have each other, and the beer.
Our good-for-nothing pals still gather here
    To booze and trample
    And set an example
From which the Golden Boy can bravely veer.

We're up, and it's a fine day in the land.
Apparently some Princess needs a hand.
    It's us she wants?
    Okay. This once.
Show us the map. This time we'll understand.

Don't Waste Your Breath

On sales or sermons at my door,
Contributions from the floor,
    Screaming things.
Wondering where the good times went,
Complaining to this Government,
    Reciting 'Kings'.

Telling fibs to Sherlock Holmes,
Games of tag with garden gnomes,
    Soliloquies.
Knock-knock jokes on a Croatian,
Great ideas for situation
    Comedies.

Asking her to reconsider
Leaving, trying to kid a kidder,
    Roundelays.
Entering for field events,
Just causes or impediments
    On wedding days.

Begging rides in backs of hearses,
Happy Birthday's other verses,
    Asking twice.
Musing on your point-blank misses,
Moaning 'This is hell' or 'This is
    Paradise.'

Offering a monk your ticket,
Using metaphors from cricket
　　When in Texas.
Telephoning during finals,
Remonstrating in urinals
　　With your Exes.

Phrases like 'Here's what I think,'
Giving up girls/smoking/drink
　　At New Year.
Asserting that all men are equal,
Settling down to write a sequel
　　To *King Lear*.

Revisions to *The Odyssey*,
Improvements on Psalm 23
　　Or hazel eyes.
Gluing back the arms on Venus,
Any other rhyme than 'penis',
　　The Turner Prize.

Interrogating diplomats,
Defining Liberal Democrats,
　　Begging to banks.
Supporting Malta's football team,
Translating King's 'I have a dream'
　　Into the Manx.

Reading verse to lesser mammals,
Tailing cats or humping camels,
　　Hectoring sheep.
Pleading with a traffic warden,
Writing things that sound like Auden
　　In his sleep.

Don't waste your breath on telling me
My purpose, point or pedigree
   Or wit or worth.
Don't waste your breath explaining how
A poem works or should do now
   You're on the Earth.

Don't waste your breath on rage, regret
Or ridicule; don't force or fret,
   Breathe easily.
Remember: every starlit suck
Is seven trillion parts good luck
   To one part me.

The Great Detectives

None can leap as far as the great detectives.
Not only can they bare the cause as if
It stripped itself in public, they can sniff
Effects it never had till now, or motives
Stuffed in coats, contemptibly denied
By those who did it, know it, and can't hide.

None can sleep as light as the great sleuths.
To them the stars are evidence, the moon
A gaping witness and the nightmares soon
Resolved into incriminating truths.
The corn of life is twisted into scenes.
Who have the time and reason have the means.

Who hangs about that drawing-room alone?
None now, where failures trot to the great chair
And ring around its ankles like a fair.
Then everything is epilogue, is known.
After the accusation's shot and stuck,
Who's left will make an innocence of luck.

No certainties like those of private eyes,
Once the detecting bug is coughed and caught:
Whatever art is made, or history taught,
What isn't Law might just as well be lies
For all the help it brings in the hot nights
Before the white steam clears and he alights.

No charm like his, no eccentricities
So crisp, authenticating and sincere.
And, as for her, who would have thought it here?
That one could solve so many with such ease?
But better turn those hooks and curious eyes
To joyful exclamations of surprise!

The truth is out with murder and with blood.
They drape across the sofas of the town.
Whatever may be used is taken down.
A friend runs into strangers in a wood.
He shrugs the shoulders that the earth has picked
To flop upon and sleep. In the next act

The corpse is quiet. Once the avenging eyes
Have gone out for each other and for good,
The guiltlessness will swell like a flash flood
And thunder as it must, where the land lies
Low and weak, then crack out to the sea
That mutters Hamlet's question endlessly.

The great detectives of our time we'll never
See at first hand, ours is a later book.
We don't know how it ends though we do look,
Climb nervously ahead to the dust cover
And peer at names. We can't expect the murder.
We must be those who don't. We're not the reader:

We have to cast about this ancient pile
Without a host, and make our plans together;
Or sleep alone and dream of one another,
And pause in all its chambers for a while,
Lift every implement, have every cause,
Be watched in silence through the double doors.

We have to know we could appear to be
Accomplice, alibi or, munching there,
The thirteenth guest who's welcome to his chair,
For how we need him in our company.
But, when the porch is darkened with the shape
Of hat and stick, of case and folded cape,

When all are drawn towards him in a room,
As shadows of suspicion fall like cards,
When some are lost and some are lost for words,
And some, forgetting, gratefully assume –
Be out of that dead chapter like the clues
He couldn't understand, so couldn't use.

We Billion Cheered

We billion cheered.
   Some threat sank in the news and disappeared.
It did because
   Currencies danced and we forgot what it was.

It rose again.
   It rose and slid towards our shore and when
It got to it,
   It laced it like a telegram. We lit

Regular fires,
   But missed it oozing along irregular wires
Towards the Smoke.
   We missed it elbowing into the harmless joke

Or dreams of our
   Loves asleep in the cots where the dolls are.
We missed it how
   You miss an o'clock passing and miss now.

We missed it where
   You miss my writing of this and I miss you there.
We missed it through
   Our eyes, lenses, screen and angle of view.

We missed it though
   It specified where it was going to go,
And when it does,
   The missing ones are ten to one to be us.

We line the shore.
    Speak of the waving dead of a waving war.
And clap a man
    For an unveiled familiar new plan.

Don't forget.
    Nothing will start that hasn't started yet.
Don't forget
    It, its friend, its foe, and its opposite.

The Furthest West

You lot got dazzled and burned
All afternoon. We two were last to arrive,
Tipsy and hand in hand
And, if they go, and they do, will be last to leave.

The rocks encroach and the Cornish sand stretches
Where we settle. This
Is the furthest west she says she has gone for ages,
Which isn't true, I think, but I say yes.

Blues emerge and blur, like the promenade sketcher
Couldn't do edges well and thought
A vague, dark and watery picture
The pricier art.

Fine constellations spoil his plan. I
Sweep them up in my right hand.
More grains in here, you know, than stars in the sky.
Yes, she says with a sniff. Other way round.

Now the sea goes quiet, straining to hear
Our shared and differing views.
Then gathers, rolling, breaking clean out of nowhere
Its only news.

The Sightseers

We sing, we lucky pirates, as we sail,
Overladen with our creaking cargo
Of eights and nines, and imagine chains of island
Zeroes up ahead. Some of us are ill, though,
And yelp and gibber of a rushing edge,
A foam of stars, the boatswain upside down
Who grins *You told me so.*
                         We draw to the rail,
Sleepless, and we wait, and, sure enough,

Behind us like our chat against the breezes,
They stir and mutter, whom we call the Sightseers,
Who stay the length of a hundred of my heartbeats.
No time at all with the Sightseers behind us.

I count the beats, it's how I'm brave enough
Not to cry out or vault the rail for terror –
I number them as years of the dim hundred
Soon to be gone: so I have them born to sunlight,
Then growing in that apple England, picked
Or fallen, then I think of them as upright,
Ideas and expectations trailing off
Across the years, and then I see them cold,
Unshockable and tired. And by the time I

Stumble in on the sixty-second heartbeat
Their eyes are red with secrets, and their heads
Are white with what is put from an honest mind,
And then they don't believe what they are seeing.
And then they are seeing nothing, and I believe

They walk on deck because they wake and sniff
Some empty space at every century's end,
Like breath gone out, or the air of the first flowers
That ever filled their eyes, as if it's starting –
They jolt from bed and hurry from their cabins

To see strange figures clutching at a rail.
We sing, we lucky pirates, as we sail.

Villagers' New Year Song

From *Wolfpit*, Act III, Scene i

The apple's eaten, the year is died,
The sun is climbing over the side,
The sparrow's flown the ocean wide,
    Remember me, forget me.

Gather in rings and part in pairs,
And ring the days and part the years,
Twinkle from another's tears,
    Remember me, forget me.

Old Year left my love for dead,
New Year see me wooed and wed,
For all was said that will be said,
    Remember me, forget me.

Cold is life but living burns,
Winter rakes but Spring returns,
Then Summer sweats till Autumn yearns,
    Remember me, forget me.

Fresh is dawn and pale and rose
With blood of Time, but no one knows
Where Time or Love or Laughter goes,
    Remember me, forget me.

The apple's eaten, the year is died,
The sun is climbing over the side,
The sparrow's flown the ocean wide,
    Remember me, forget me.

Deep Song of Us

The slowness of this thought: the rocky street.
The white and slowness of these fingers: meat
   Afloat. The utterable word
   Gulped, the plausible self
Clammed, in hiding. Booms of a heart unheard
   Impel this head, this whole head,
      Towards a gulf.

High over, far below, the being beats
Onwards, habited, drummed, and light repeats
   It isn't its opposite.
   The seconds reel along
On six enclosing films, and the next minute
   Forms into a room, this room,
      For this song.

We are the underwater here, the cold
Progressors from elsewhere, from gaps in an old
   Silence to new gaps
   In a fresh silence: still,
We eat, will not unsip the monster sips
   Of the wide blue, the narrow blue
      Unbreathing chill.

Look how the brown bewitcher looms into view,
Startled but only startled by how you
   Stared at her. The drapes
   Settle across that sight.
Along the world's great side three fluttering shapes
   Could be tracking us. Could be luring us.
      Could bite.

We are the underwater. Do you blame us?
Do you know us? Do you really. Name us.
　　Tell us by our twin
　　Terrors: one, these yellow
Gleaming aliens hauling our kind in,
　　The spit of us, the salt of us,
　　　Our fellow;

Then, rainbow-rimmed, the lidding placid sky,
Unswallowable except to surface and die
　　On heaven sauced with thick
　　Floats. We agree hell
The better deal, and lump together, sick.
　　I reckon this. You reckon this.
　　　It's just as well,

For the front line is a horror. Now all lines
Are horrors: a child dapples, flashes, shines –
　　We say Get Down. Dive.
　　Plunge and forget, yawn
That jaw then sip in shadow, still alive,
　　Sunlight-proof. Midnight-proof.
　　　Immune to dawn.

We hit the bottom, watch our gravely ill
Lug themselves towards us, and we know we'll
　　Kick to the green middle,
　　Hang out there for a spell,
An inturned, peering, recognizing huddle:
　　You three and me. You six and me.
　　　What do we tell –

Catch my eyes I tell an embedded tale
Of one and another one, female and male
　　Slipped together: Ring-
　　And-Finger. This goes down
In silence by our firesides but we sing
　　A song then. The song then.
　　　Around our town.

We sing where the whole schools of the sky-eyed green
Chew, reminded. We sing by the machine
   That somersaulted slowly,
   Falling through everything,
Chains elbowing down and past our holy
   Quiet, landing in quiet,
     Balancing,

And finally caving over into the sand.
We sing by what was a ship, and what a hand.
   We sing where light and smell
   Mean danger and the other,
And call our hell a heaven for a hell.
   We repeat bits. We repeat bits
     To one another.

I save my best bass for the brown bewitcher
When she comes, but when she does I'll watch her
   In deep, wide hunger
   And lose my place, I know.
And not a few will hear my Ring-and-Finger
   And doubt it, doubt I believe it.
     I do, though.

Inaudible, we sing. Misunderstood
We do the seven actions. If you only could
   See us you would know,
   Over the oil in the sky,
Where both our diehards and our light dead go,
   Where you paint us, where you want us,
     Where you don't die,

Where you walk on, your each mutter a scream
To our ears, your scream a wordless scream,
   Our colours yours, though yours
   We blend to the one lime,
Your toxin steeping down into our pores
   Forever, to ring forever,
     Ingested time:

You would know that – Hunt us, clouds will clear.
Catch us, one held dear will hold you dear.
    Roast us, we will trust.
    Waste us in the heaven
You hope is hell, and we shall be at rest.
    Do what you do. Whatever you do,
        You stay forgiven.

Errand Boy

To amble on on the brightening, clouding
pavement to happen to pass whom he wants,
    innocently, to pass involves
passing his home with feigned indifference
and moving on, nowhere left to be heading.

She is the brown bare-armed au pair,
her charges holding her hands. Though he really
    means his major smile at them,
it is all in his own and other way fairly
for her, and their voices are English and clear

as they fade, hers neither as it also fades.
And now he's stuck on an imaginary errand, which
    seems to be suddenly unimportant
from the way he slows down and checks his watch
then monitors interesting forming clouds.

Watching Over

Elated by ourselves, we shift and slip –
Mouths open with the memory of a kiss –
Parting in two to sleep, and if it's mine

Then that was it, that break above, and now
It's yours I wake to witness your unknowing
Our love and all you know.
                         Some ancient will,
Though night is safe and quiet here, commands
You be watched over now, and, to that end,
Exacerbates the wind and whipping rains,
Or amplifies the howls of animals
To make my waking watchful and tense,
Though for a thousand miles there is no mind
To hurt you, nor one raindrop on the wind.

Stargazing

The night is fine and dry. It falls and spreads
the cold sky with a million opposites
that, for a spell, seem like a million souls
and soon, none, and then, for what seems a long time,
one. Then of course it spins. What is better to do
than string out over the infinite dead spaces
the ancient beasts and spearmen of the human
mind, and, if not the real ones, new ones?

But, try making them clear to one you love –
whoever is standing by you is one you love
when pinioned by the stars – you will find it quite
impossible, but like her more for thinking
she sees that constellation.

After the wave of pain, you will turn to her
and, in an instant, change the universe
to a sky you were glad you came outside to see.

This is the act of all the descended gods
of every age and creed: to weary of all
that never ends, to take a human hand,
and go back into the house.

Mick Imlah

Goldilocks

This is a story about the possession of beds.
It begins at the foot of a staircase in Oxford, one midnight,
When (since my flat in the suburbs of London entailed
A fiancée whose claims I did not have the nerve to evict)

I found myself grateful for climbing alone on a spiral
To sleep I could call with assurance exclusively mine;
For there was the name on the oak that the Lodge had
    assigned
Till the morning to me (how everything tends to its place!)

And flushed with the pleasing (if not unexpected) success
Of the paper on 'Systems of Adult-to-Infant Regression'
With which the Young Fireball had earlier baffled his
    betters
At the Annual Excuse for Genetics to let down its ringlets,

I'd just sniggered slightly (pushing the unlocked door
Of the room where I thought there was nothing of mine
    to protect)
To observe that my theory, so impudent in its address
To the Masters of Foetal Design and their perfect disciples,

Was rubbish – and leant to unfasten the window a notch –
When I suddenly grasped with aversion before I could see it
The fact that the bed in the corner directly behind me
Had somebody in it. A little ginger chap,

Of the sort anthropologists group in the genus of *tramp*,
Was swaddled, as though with an eye to the state of the sheets,
With half of his horrible self in the pouch of the bedspread
And half (both his raggled and poisonous trouser-legs) out;

Whose snore, like the rattle of bronchial stones in a bucket,
Resounded the length and the depth and the breadth of the problem
Of how to establish in safety a climate conducive
To kicking him out – till at last I could suffer no longer

The sight of his bundle of curls on my pillow, proof
That even the worst of us look in our sleep like the angels
Except for a few. I closed to within a yard
And woke him, with a curt hurrahing sound.

And he reared in horror, like somebody late for work
Or a débutante subtly apprised of a welcome outstayed,
To demand (not of me, but more of the dreary familiar
Who exercised in its different styles the world's

Habit of persecution, and prodded him now)
Phit time is it? – so you'd think that it made any difference –
So you'd think after all that the berth had a rota attached
And Ginger was wise to some cynical act of encroachment;

But when, with a plausible echo of fatherly firmness,
I answered, 'It's bedtime' – he popped out and stood in a shiver,
And the released smell of his timid existence swirled
Like bracing coffee between our dissimilar stances.

Was there a dim recollection of tenement stairways
And jam and the Rangers possessed him, and sounded a
    moment
In creaks of remorse? 'Ah'm sorry, son – Ah couldnae tell
They'd hae a wee boy sleepin here – ye know?'

(And I saw what a file of degradations queued
In his brown past, to explain how Jocky there
Could make me out to be innocent and wee:
As if to be wee was not to be dying of drink;

As if to be innocent meant that you still belonged
Where beds were made for one in particular.)
Still, the lifespan of sociable feelings is shortest of all
In the breast of the migrant Clydesider; and soon he relapsed

Into patterns of favourite self-pitying sentiments. 'Son –
Ah'm warse than – Ah cannae, ye know? Ah'm off tae ma
    dandy!
Ah've done a wee josie – aye, wheesh! – it's warse what
    Ah'm gettin –
Aye – warse!' And again the appeal to heredity – 'Son.'

(In the course of his speech, the impostor had gradually
    settled
Back on the bed, and extended as visual aids
His knocked-about knuckles; tattooed with indelible
    foresight
On one set of these was the purple imperative SAVE.)

Now I'm keen for us all to be just as much worse as we
    want,
In our own time and space – but not, after midnight, in
    my bed;
And to keep his inertia at bay, I went for the parasite,
Scuttling him off with a shout and the push of a boot

That reminded his ribs I suppose of a Maryhill barman's,
Until I had driven him out of the door and his cough
Could be heard to deteriorate under a clock in the landing.
(Och, if he'd known *I* was Scottish! Then I'd have got it.)

(*

But of course he came back in the night, when I dreamed
    I was coughing
And he stood by the door in the composite guise of a woman –
A mother, a doting landlady, a shadowy wife –
Sleepless as always, relieved none the less to have found me,

Or half relieved – given what I had become;
Saying – 'It's just from the coughing and so on I wondered
If maybe a tramp had got into your bedroom' – and then,
Disappointedly: 'Couldn't you spare a wee thought for
     your dad?'

(I thought I was dreaming again on the train in the morning
To hear at my shoulder, before I had properly settled,
'Excuse me – is this seat taken?' spastically spoken;
But it wasn't our friend that I humoured through Didcot,
     and Reading,

No, but an anoracked spotter of diesels from Sheffield
Whose mind was apparently out in the sidings at Crewe:
Only one more in a world of unwanted connections,
Who waved like a child when I fled for the toilet at Ealing.)

                              *

This is my gloss on the story of Goldilocks. Note:
It uncovers a naked and difficult thought about beds,
Namely, that seldom again will there ever be one
With only you in it; take that however you will.

Tusking

In Africa once
A herd of Harrow
Elephants strayed
Far from their bunks;
Leather, they laid
Their costly trunks
And ears of felt
Down on the Veldt.

All forgot
The creep of dusk;
A moonbeam stole
Along each tusk:
Snores and sighs.
Oh, foolish boys!
The English elephant
Never lies!

*

In the night-time, lithe
Shadows with little
Glinting teeth
Whisked tusks away;
Drew through the dark
Branches of ivory,
Made a great hue
On their rapid run.

Hunters, at home
They curl up the bare
Soles of their feet
With piano-pleasure;
Sammy plays
A massacre song
With the notes wrong
On Massa's baby.

*

Out in the bush
Is silence now:
Savannah seas
Have islands now,
Smelly land-masses,
Bloody, cold,
Disfigured places
With fly-blown faces;

And each of us rests
After his fashion:
Elephant, English,
Butcher, Bushman;
Now only the herding
Boy in a singlet
Worries his goat
With a peaceful prod.

*

But if, one night
As you stroll the verandah
Observing with wonder
The place of the white
Stars in the universe,
Brilliant, and clear,
Sipping your whisky
And pissed with fear

You happen to hear
Over the tinkle
Of ice and Schubert
A sawing – a drilling –
The bellow and trump
Of a vast pain –
Pity the hulks!
Play it again!

Visiting St Anthony

'*St Anthony's Bunker*, fifty miles by jeep;
Not often touristed, and very cheap;
The humble desert home of ANTHONY,
Oldest of human beings, and a saint.'

I don't remember what I half expected
When I picked that xeroxed advert from the rest
And made my booking, to the mild surprise
Of the agent, in his shuttered, dingy room;

Long tracts of beard, perhaps, on a bony
Story-teller; or skin to prod, with a pig
Fast at one ankle; but I don't remember.
We came upon it after hours of sand.

'Mister,' the guide implored, the truck slowing,
'The saint is at his books . . .' I smelt a rat;
And sure enough, we dwindled to a stop
At what he called 'respectful' yards away

From terror, or complaint, before a sign
Whose motto's paint dribbled sarcastically:
AS THE FISH REMOVED FROM WATER SLOWLY DIES
SO DOES THE MONK WHO WANDERS FROM HIS CELL

– What 'cell'? – What pilgrim dared they hope to fool
By the bivouac of planks that Tuesday's hands
Had scrambled up to scarcely overlook
Miles of a wasted journey? Or plonked on top,

What chance that the poor beggar bound to a stool
With half a hymnal stuffed between his knees
Couldn't be dead? It wasn't cloth, but wire
That kept him blindfold, and his skull intact,

And nothing surgical that plugged the holes
Where saints have eyes. I measured up the fraud:
They'd raked this load of maggots from his thin
Pittance of rest, for my few quid – Arabs!

So much the worse my second shock. I saw
The skull, beneath its ragged hood of flesh,
Bend, like a monk's white face, as if to read;
And when, at once, it buckled and recoiled

There came a foul noise, like the waking cry
Of dogs behind the oil-drums of his door
And that was all; the pages fluttered over
Like profit counted; and the guide resumed.

'The chain leads to the Saint's devoted PIG,
Which is a thing like Mary's little lamb
Or the love of God for every hopeless man,
Whose patience is so gross, it will survive

Although the pig is very old, for a pig –
Even as old as Master Anthony.'
But there was no pig to be seen, anywhere,
Of any age, unless that hump of flies –

And I don't suppose we'd parked for a minute, before
I motioned to the guide to turn for town;
Who thought me scared, no doubt, but knew the tomb,
And was himself no chicken, as he said.

Silver

Silver in block or chain
Will not sustain
    The nameless slaves
    Who row it through the waves

As long as the old, crude
Hallmark tattooed
    On every chest
    Proclaims them second-best.

Wherever the ship may steer
They face the rear;
    What lies in store
    Is untransmuted ore.

*

Breaking into the bungalow, we found
His last meal full of maggots on the cooker,
Four hundred and forty-six pounds in pound notes
In various vases and drawers,
And a bowls cup from the fifties, silvery-brown,
By the tin of Duraglit –
He had been polishing it.

Lee Ho Fook's

What brought the Chinaman down to the building-site? Ah, it
  was Fate;
And Fate in the scaffolding kicked from its cradle the vat,
Thirty foot over his dithering head, of boiling and thunderous tea.
Who was on hand, though, to rush from his post and manhandle
  the fellow
(Then of a frightened, diminutive, immigrant state of fragility)
Into a sheltering barrow, the moment the day's brew exploded
Exactly where seconds before he'd been staring and dreaming
  of mountains
And seagulls and sails in the harbour? Charlie Wood.

The building-site is buildings now, the Cannon Street Office
Of the Hong Kong and Cantonese Bank – and all would be
  buried beneath
Were it not for the Chinaman's blur of cross-cultural gratitude:
'You have saved my life. The least I can do in return
Is to ask you to dine as my guest in my fabulous restaurant
Whenever you will.' 'Well thanks very much,' says Charlie –
'I might take you up on that offer.' – Back to the grit and the grind;
Thinking, though, *Tell you what, Charlie Boy, could be a bit of a bonus!*

Indeed, while the mind of this builder was normally dark,
And dripping with flesh, and unwholesome, infested, and spotty,
  a shaft
Of purest sunshine scored suddenly over the tracks as he
  pondered his luck;
And a sluice and an avalanche opened of rice and prawns like
  the coins in *The Golden Shot*,

Churning and pouring forever and all of it aimed at his lap;
Which drew him away from the mix of cement he was feeding
And up in a daze to the Works hut, and on through a dozen
    or more
Inscrutable *Yellow Pages* – well, it would take him a couple of
    tea-breaks . . .

Years pass. And the tiny impulse of distaste Lee had felt
At his saviour's first beaming appearance and chirpy request for
    a knife and fork
Has swollen; of late it resembles a sort of unsociable illness
That has to be kept in check by a sidling withdrawal to the stairs
Whenever his own lucky star, with its multiple coatings of
    yesterday's earth,
Comes rollicking in for the freebies – as often as three times a week.
(Something is fouling the lock in the door to his dream of
    new premises;
Something as fixed as the bambooey bulge in Charlie Wood's cheek.)

So Charlie is left to chew over the Chinaman's lapses of honour
And nibble at rightful reprisals: *When his highness emerges at last*
To slide me as ever the ready-paid bill on a saucer
(*Disguising by this, he supposes, his part of the bargain*)
What if I dashed this half-cup of their pissy tea at him –
Out of the blue, to remind him why Woodsy is here?
– Or when they've been keeping me waiting an hour for the soup, to come
    out with it –
Oy, son, I had you in a barrow once – *instead of my usual?*

Clio's

Am I to be blamed for the state of it now? – Surely not –
Her poor wee fractured soul that I loved for its lightness
    and left?
Now she rings up pathetically, not to make claims of me,
Only to be in her wild way solicitous:
'Do you know of a restaurant called *Clio's* – or something
    like that –
At number *forty-three* in its road or street, – and the owner
Is beautiful, rich and Italian – you see, I dreamt of it,
And I can't relax without telling you never to go there,
Divining, somehow, that for you the place is *danger* –'

(But I dine at Clio's every night, poor lamb.)

from THE DRINKING RACE

STARTER'S ORDERS

These warless days
Men without women
Thirst for the means
To waste themselves;

It's in the blood.
Their fathers worked
And Grandad breasted
A barbed tape;

But now where the girls
Are sick of courage
Men without hope
Of a job, or a bayonet,

Muster like champions
Under a canopy,
Over a barrel,
Primed for the slaughter;

Fit to pursue
Illness, dishonour,
And sponsored to boot.
Gentlemen, swallow!

STRANGE MEETING

As I walked down towards the Drinking Race
I overtook one combatant, whose legs
Wandered abandoned under a wet face
Rubbed ruby-red by life's abrasive dregs.

He'd jumped the gun over the rest of them
And looked a certain finalist, when he slowed
To clear his throat of the obstructive phlegm
And hailed me, as I tried to cross the road.

'You coward! You! Come here!' (He took a draught
And what he drank came straight back through his nose)
'Don't you appreciate the drinker's craft?
Why won't you stop and sup with us old pros?'

When I declined, he straightened for a spell
On his best leg, and spat from this strange stance
Like a heron proud of its own repulsive smell
Or furious at a biped's arrogance:

'With better luck, I'd catch you in a fight
Or institutional combat at the bars,
And you wouldn't know if it was day or night
For the ringing in your ears, and the seeing stars;

But meantime – that's unless you'd care to part
With twenty pence?' (I smirked) '– Meantime' (his face
Drew far too close) 'You have an evening's start,
And meet me downstairs at the Drinking Race!'

HALL OF FAME

It seemed that from the beer-tent I escaped
Down some profound depression, where they kept

Silent the damaged and the down-and-out.
A sergeant rang the bell for them to eat,

That being the hour appointed; but the failures
Who shuffled from the darkness on all fours

Had burned away their appetite for solids
And only a couple accepted watery salads

To sip at on their disinfected bunks.
These were the veterans of such bloody banquets

Eternal headaches hurt them, and still hurt;
'Hey soldier!' I called at one I seemed to hate

Who was sitting helpless in his vest and pants
Over a tray of flat insipid pints:

'Didn't I see you when you were so pissed
On the road here, that a mug of whisky passed

Straight back out of your nostrils as you drank?
Tell me, how did a soldier get that drunk?

And how did you fare later?' Out of luck
He shed his numbered shorts and made me look

At something that I wished I had not seen,
The ruined arse-hole, flapping, crudely sewn,

Through which he spoke: 'After the rout – I lost,
I think, or won – came either first or last –

'They bore me up, oblivious to my wound,
On eager shoulders; before they could be warned,

'With a loud noise, the crap larruped down my leg.
Now every Christmas I raise half a lager

'To absent friends; and absent is the word,
For nobody loves me in the Drinking Ward

'Or brings me chocolates or forget-me-nots . . .'
So moaning he withdrew; the last three notes

Blew like reveille from their fading source.

Abortion

I woke the Monday after, feeling shabby
In a ship's bed, cramped in the head with the sense
That falls in private on forgetfulness
Of parties, that of someone's shame at me;

But waiting, I began to guess, would lick me
Properly into shape. Uncurled at noon,
Dry as a Dead Sea Scroll, I rose and wobbled
Blank about the cabin like a reclaimed monster

Learning to eat; and through a glassy disk
Saw even passage, sun, unpoisoning sea,
And heard the call of sea-birds hosting me
To port, and hatched an eagerness for dusk

And drink, and company. And though I dozed again,
The clock had just snored twice without alarm
When (and I thought I was dreaming) a chink
Of cups began, like washing-up:

Then with only that warning the plates
Shook on my shelves which collapsed and smashed them,
And in the immediate stillness I felt as though someone
Was sitting behind me with news of disaster.

*

Have you ever heard a noise that you think
Is unearthly (especially when you're half asleep)
But when you get it into focus it's only
Them snoring, or your neighbour revving up?

Well that's how this whirring began,
Like something familiar mistaken, becoming
As I struggled to call it a pump or the cistern
Neither, nothing else, and very loud,

Till sailors' boasts fell silent in the spray.
When we took the first buffet I dropped
My pointless jacket and almost at once
I was doubled-up in air but couldn't breathe,

And dizzy I saw an experiment
With magnets, me the broken one,
A horseshoe facing down,
Sucked up. I passed clean out

And was lucky to survive; the boat
Melted in blood, but I stiffened safely,
A rabbit's foot, gristly
In someone's cabinet.

Cockney

How heightened the taste! – of champagne at the piano; of little
    side-kisses to tickle the fancy
At the party to mark our sarcastic account of the overblown
    Mass of the Masses by Finzi
(An aristocrat who betrayed what he stood for and set up in
    Bow with his matchgirl fiancée);

Moreover, the skit I had chosen to grace the occasion ('*My Way*
    – in the Setting for Tuba by Mahler')
Had even the Previns in generous stitches (it seemed an
    acceptable social *milieu*
If only because it was something like six million light years
    away from the planet of Millwall)

When the buffet arrived; and as we applauded the *crudités* carved
    into miniature flats and sharps
There crept into mind for a desperate moment the ghost of me
    mum shuffling back from the shops
With a Saturday treat – 'Look! We got sausages, beans, an' *chips*!'

So I mentally told her to stuff it, and turned, with a shivering
    reflex of anger
To harangue a superior brace of brunettes for their preference
    of Verdi to Wagner;
But again she appeared at the door, with the salt and the sacred
    vinegar

And I was reclaimed. 'You!' she demanded, 'You who last
    month in the Seychelles
Took drinks with a Marquess, and studded the spine of Lucinda
    with seashells –
You are the same little boy that I sent out in winter with
    Cockney inscribed on your satchel!'

And as she dispersed, one or two of my neighbours were
    squinting at me as you do a bad odour,
And even my friendly advances were met by a flurry of coughs
    and a mutter of *Oh, dear* –
For try as I might I just couldn't assemble the sounds that came
    out in a delicate order:

ALL ROYT MOY SAHN! HA'S YOR FARVAH?
LEN YOU TEN NOWTS? – CALL IT A FOIVAH!
TRAVELLED IN TEE-ASCANY? – DO ME A FIVAH!

And worse was to follow. For over this bleak ostinato of base-
    born vowels
I detected the faraway strains of a disco remix of 'The Dance of
    the Seven Veils'
And felt the lads egging me on to enact what a tug at the
    Seventh reveals –

Yes, down came the pants of old Rotherhithe's rugged Salomé,
And pointing it straight at the toff who was leading the charge
    to assail me
Out of my shirtfront I prodded two thirds of a purple
    salami . . .

*

Sometimes, there's a song in my head as I sit down at tea, and I
    know what the tune is
But can't do the words. And when I get tired of the humming,
    it's off down to Terry's, or Tony's,
A couple of pints, then across to the club till it closes, for
    snooker with Pakistanis.

MOUNTAINS

SNOWDONIAN

At the start of our climbing career
Each had his flask, his blue cagoule
And a uniform will to be first
In the sprint to the peak;
Nobody thought it was steep
Or fell far out of step.

So, back at the gabled hostel,
There were coffee and biscuits, a perfect
Unnecessary roll-call,
Viollet, Wavering,
White, Wood,
And no weak link exposed;

Though on the downward scree
Slipping and dying in jest
Twyford (2Y) had spotted a single
Classic sure-foot, bearded goat
Lost to the herd, broken-backed
Among heathery boulders.

ALPINE

Stranded at base
When the four had gone
To grow for a gown
Frost's blue fur,

On my mind's reel
I seemed to follow
Their blurrying through
The storm's crackle

Till, wavering,
White against white,
They shivered off the screen
Like watermarks . . .

Now in the sun
Twisting blue
Daisies across
Finger and thumb,

I think I hear one
Of the frayed chain
Or the ghost of one
Baring bad gifts:

'Here are my hands'
(I think I see them)
'Violet and white
And hard as wood.'

HIMALAYAN
Concern about our provisions was to cost us many sleepless nights.
            – Sir John Hunt

Roof of the world; rumble of avalanche; something attacking
The splintering walls of our matchstick lodge with a
 vengeance;
And all I could glimpse from the sleeping bag (face to the
 floorboards'
Powdery glass) was a snowdrift of beans, and a Nescafé label –
These were the last of our rations exploding about us!

(And it struck me again, in the hail from a cereal packet,
As when the kitchen in Ballater crackled with fire
From a fault in the toaster, the everyday nature of danger;
When even our comforts can turn, and our breakfast itself
Come in volleys against us.) And then he was there: there,
   at the door –

There, with his featureless face at a gap in the ceiling –
Abominable, the Monster of the Slope,
Furry with frost, in the guise of a ghastly storeman:
'Get off my mountain. Get off my world.'
– Slapping huge coffee-jars into our lodge.

POLAR
Sometimes all Nature seems for us, sometimes against.
                                              – Edward Whymper

. . . For perhaps twenty minutes we stood petrified in the darkness as an innumerable dense flock of penguins swept over us, blotting out the sun and the sky, all inclined upwards as though in an aerial charge at the summit . . .

. . . The final push has been postponed again, in the wake of a horrid discovery. After good progress earlier this morning, we had slowed somewhat by noon when Hislop, who was leading, let out a series of screams, like a man who has found his skin covered with unexpected creatures. I crabbed as quickly as possible to his assistance, and though I could not understand him at first, he managed to convey by gestures that he had scraped his boot with a pick, and found *beaks*. I checked my own footing, and examined the lines of a ridge above, where the coating of blackish ice petered out like slush; and in a moment it became unpleasantly clear to me that we had been climbing in the mist on a sort of frosted mud made of penguins, for miles and miles.

. . . Morphine! and monstrous dreams . . . All nature for us or against us. I have no pictures of that bed of penguins.

?

Because it isn't there . . . I slipped and fell
A thousand feet; woke with my boots on

And the camp doctor's hand weighing my wrist
As he said gently, son, your nerve has gone.

Birthmark

On my decline, a millipede
Helped me to keep count;
For every time I slipped a foot
Further down the mountain

She'd leave a tiny, cast-off limb
Of crimson on my cheek
As if to say –
You're hurting us both, Mick . . .

I saw in this gradual sacrifice
No end of merriment:
A broken vein or two; hardly
Memento mori.

This thousandth morning after, though
(Or thousand-and-first)
I miss her, and a bedside mirror
Bellows the worst –

A big, new, bilberry birthmark, stamped
From ear to livid ear,
Her whole body of blood's
Untimely smear.

She must have found, shaking her sock
For warnings, that the hoard was spent,
And had to stain me with her death
To show what she meant:

That it's as bad to fall astray
As to start from the wrong place.
Now I have earned the purple face.
It won't go away.

Past Caring

As a ship
Sees only the tip
Of the ice's pyramid
That has already scraped her bows,
We'd glimpsed that drink was something you overdid;
Now after the wreck I sift the damage you'd stowed in the house.

Eyes glazed
I fumble, amazed,
Through mounds of knickers and slips,
Extracting the bottles you'd buried there; these
I hump in their binbags, clashing against my knees
To the 'Bottlebank', by the public baths; it takes four trips.

The gin!
No wonder you're thin;
Hundreds of bottles of gin;
And feeding them singly into the ring
My arm grows weary from shifting the bottles of gin;
– A numbing collection of lots of exactly the same thing.

You were vain
As you went down the drain;
Why else would you lay up this hoard
If it wasn't one day to take stock as I'm doing
Of what an almighty amount you had taken on board?
And here am I turning your trophies to scrap at an illicit viewing!

A smear
of lipstick, here –
Like the kiss on a valentine;
And sniffing the neck I feel suddenly near to you,
For what it gives off is your smell, if we kissed any time,
And it wasn't a cheap perfume – but the only thing properly dear to you.

Next week
If you're not past caring
They may let you out for an airing,
– To slump in your armchair, too burgled to speak,
The fish out of water that stubbornly stays but the more fish;
– Then how shall we drag the treasure you were back to the surface?

AFTERLIVES OF THE POETS

I   IN MEMORIAM ALFRED LORD TENNYSON
d. 6 October 1892

> I remember once in London the realization coming over me, of the whole of its inhabitants lying horizontal a hundred years hence.
> – Tennyson, quoted in Audrey Tennyson's notebook

No one remembers you at all.
　　Even that shower of Cockney shrimps
　　Whose fathers hoisted them to glimpse
Your corpse's progress down Whitehall

Have soiled the till and lain beneath:
　　While the last maid you kissed with feeling
　　Is staring at the eternal ceiling
And has no tongue between her teeth.

Now sanctified are your remains:
　　The poems; Hallam's obedient book;
　　The photographs your neighbour took
Of an old Jesus with food stains;

The rest is dressed up decently
　　And drowned, as surely as your son's
　　Untimely coffin, that flashed once
And slipped into the Indian Sea.

You are not here; you cannot fall.
　　So let the mighty organ blare!
　　While we, who plainly were not there
Construct this fake memorial.

*

In the hope of finding something that might flesh out my phantom Tennyson centenary project, my girlfriend drove me one evening down to Aldworth, in Sussex, the poet's second home and the closest of his haunts to London. We had read of the new owner's extreme hostility to visitors, but she wasn't deterred, on my behalf, by the height of the gate, nor by the notice of watchdogs. So I followed her suggestion to break into the garden, and carried the torch down a path which gave me a dim view of the front of the house, from about 50 metres, across a minefield of lilies and a steaming pond, and absorbed this for a minute before heading back to join her on the drive. But even as my feet landed again on neutral gravel, she screamed – not at the flash of what seemed like lightning, but at something on my blind side it must have lit up. So I turned to confront what I guessed in that instant was either our man with a shotgun or an earlier intruder strung up by his heels.

*

Cannot you, as a friend of Mr Tennyson, prevent his making such a hideous exhibition of himself as he has been doing for the last three months? . . . I thought there was a law against indecent exposure.

– Swinburne to Lord Houghton

When fifteen men were charged at Bow Street Court on Monday after a disturbance around Eros, in Piccadilly Circus, it was mentioned in court that one of them claimed to be Lord Tennyson. Lord Tennyson wishes to state that the man was not in fact Lord Tennyson, and has no connections with him, and that he does not know him.

– *The Times*, 1 January 1948

*

I knew him at once – for a student, or out-of-work actor, or worse,
With Tennyson's frock and fedora, and a volume of Tennyson's verse,
But even the mouldiest music-hall turn would be sunk from the start
By a stature at least seven inches too short for the Laureate's part.
This was a bloke whose kraken had woken for years twice a night
In some shallow provincial canal; and when he began to recite,
The personal touch of the door-to-door salesman could never obscure
That this was the fiftieth one-to-one Tennyson show of the tour.
'Mr Imlah! The warmest of greetings, good sir, from myself and the Queen!
I'm Alfred, Lord Tennyson – dare I suggest that you know who I mean?
So relax – and unlatch the front gates of your mind – for tonight I arrive
To proclaim as I did once before – The Dead Are Not Dead But Alive!'

*

> . . . the full, the monstrous demonstration that Tennyson was not
> Tennysonian.
>
> – Henry James, *The Middle Years*

(Oscar Browning introduces himself)
   O. BROWNING: I am Browning.
   TENNYSON: No you're not.

> – E. F. Benson, *As We Were*

(T. on a portrait of the dead Dickens)
   This is the most extraordinary drawing. It is exactly like myself.

*

'The trick of the afterlife is – that what you sign up for, you get,
And that as in the case of Tithonus this is often a source of regret.
Ours is a sepia parlour, a club without pipes or the port
Half full of identical males, where Her Majesty still holds court.
As we strut in our standardized jacket with beards on our standardized face,
Dickens and Grace and myself are called the Three Graces – by Grace.
This isn't the Hilton on High, there's no night-club or pool-with-jacuzzi –

You can walk in the garden with Gladstone, or stand at the
        piano with Pusey.
And yet, while we keep the old pastimes, we keep the old dread:
And that, for our sins, is an absolute terror of being dead,
For the truly immortal are scarce as the hairs on Arthur Clough's head,
And Darwin reminds us, you've got to look after your name
        to survive –
You rest on your laurels, you're gone with the Shadwells and
        Cibber and Clive.
These days we can hardly get four for bridge; I've seen the departure
Of Lytton – well, granted – but *Manning*, by God, and *Macaulay*,
        and *Archer*!
They're all cast over the margin and into the beggarly throng
Who bray for biography, down in the darkness, all the night long.
My Arthur – poor angel, I did what I could – I see in fits:
His wings gone limp with disuse, and the plumage in ribbons where bits
Of his carcass stick out like spokes of a broken and bandaged umbrella.
His features appear where he gnaws at the grille of his terrible cellar,
Fading and growing and fading again with never a sound,
And but for my friendship his luminous half-life would choke
        underground.

Tonight there was dancing in heaven – jigs with Elizabeth Siddal.
But after an hour on the fringe of events, and her in the middle,
I suddenly hated the uniform steps and the scrape of the fiddle,
And staggered out dizzily into the thick of the alien stars,
Shouting my name, till Hesperus fetched me in one of her cars
And dropped me on Earth for the evening. I'm saved. And to
        hell with the distance –
There's times when you've got to get out amongst folk to
        promote your existence.'
– And now from the folds of his frock-coat he brought out the
        book and affected
A cartoon myopia, cribbed from its cover (the Penguin *Selected*) –
'And so to that end it's my pleasure to read to you – starting with *Maud*.

I hate – ' but I couldn't take more of this, be it delusion or
     fraud,
So I hushed him abruptly and fished out a quid for the in-
     patients' kitty
And gathered my girlfriend to make our way back to her car
     and the city –
Casting a jibe at him over my shoulder – 'You're not Lord
     Tennyson' –
And catching the small, disembodied retort, 'Well, neither's
     Lord Tennyson.'

*

Tennyson at a séance –
A great poet, lest we forget,
And certainly one of the most haunted –
Before all the others had settled,
Cried out in a cracked voice,
'Are you my boy Lionel?' – and got
Not
The reply that he wanted.

II 'B.V.'

(The story of James Thomson (1834–82), the author of *The City of Dreadful Night*, is told in Tom Leonard's book *Places of the Mind*. Thomson was born in Port Glasgow but removed aged six to London, where he was educated in an institution for Scottish orphans. An alcoholic, he was 'discharged with disgrace' from his first post as an army schoolmaster, and thereafter lived as a lodger in a succession of single rooms in Pimlico, scraping an irregular income from contributions to journals like *Cope's Tobacco Plant*. He never published under his own name, preferring the pseudonym 'B.V.'; and in one fit of self-disgust burned all his personal papers as he approached what he wrongly thought was the midpoint of his life, his thirty-fifth birthday. Twelve years on, offered a belated chance by friends, the Barrs (two brothers and a sister), to recover himself in the Leicestershire countryside, he relapsed instead into one last 'dreadful night' in the city, and died of a broken blood vessel in his bowel a few weeks later.

An uncompromising free-thinker, the constant theme of Thomson's serious verse is the impossibility of an afterlife.)

*

If circumstances had been smoother and brighter about him . . . he would have had what was much needed in his case, a more spacious home.

— George Meredith, letter to Henry Salt, 1 September 1888

The Walker

Had I but means and a free mind
    You'd never tie me to one bed
For I should wander unconfined
    And virgin paths should feel my tread

  — James Thomson, unpublished fragment, notebook, Dobell MS

Things being worse, while I must creep
    Each evening back to Pimlico
Still I can leap before I sleep
    Through Hampstead Heath, or Barnes, or Bow;

Unless THE CLOUD resumes its place
    And the rains rain gutterly;
For then I pace my given space –
    Three by four, four by three –

And feel akin to the caged creatures
    In Regent's Park: to the roofed-in
Eagle with the impacted features,
    Or the brown bear in his bear-bin

Who rocks upon a yard of slate
    With room for three of his four paws,
Shifting his weight to simulate
    The bearing of the thing he was.

 Leicestershire County Council
Committed to equality of opportunity

IN ASSOCIATION WITH THE ARTS COUNCIL OF GREAT BRITAIN

Running Fox Project

WRITER-IN-RESIDENCE

Applications are invited from published authors of poetry
or fiction for the post of Writer-in-Residence with the Running
Fox Project, based at the Belle Vue Unit for Displaced Persons
in the heart of the Charnwood Forest. The successful applicant
will demonstrate an enthusiasm and aptitude for helping the
homeless to express themselves. The remuneration is £6,000 for
a twelve-month assignment.

Guardian, 26 September 1994

An Invitation

Friend, come and stay awhile; Miss Barrs and I
   Crave the refreshment of your company;
And if, of late, your old unhappiness
   Has made you sick, better to convalesce
Where we can nourish you with country things,
   Like Leicester beans and bacon – 'food of kings'
And the best smell the commoner ever smelt;
   Pork pies from Melton Mowbray, pies that melt
Crust, meat and jelly, in the crowded mouth;
   Pickles from Branston Valley to the south;
Stilton, or *Quenby*, judged 'the greatest cheese
   In all the world' by local authorities;
And the fat capon from our farmyard, done
   In wine and lemon – or lemon and tarragon.
Thence to the [non-] smoking room, where we may pass
   Hours with the couplet rather than the glass,
And put old Horace right ('No poem lasts long
   That hath been writ on *aqua*' – doubly wrong,
Steeped as he was in the Pierian Spring);
   And last, with nightcaps on our heads, we'll sing,
Accompanied purely by my father's daughter,
   To prove the lyric qualities of water.

Homely amusements! – and they may read mild
   To one whose nature has run wholly wild;
But look: you have a thousand acres here
   Of fern and gorse, and ancient oak, and deer
To ramble where you will; and in these grounds
   Your spirit may shake off the ghostly hounds
That haunt you into illness. Come, be calm;
   Do odd jobs, if you like, around the farm,
Feeding the chickens, or collecting wood;
   And if your pledge of abstinence holds good,

The Fates may yet extend their benisons
   And *Thomson*'s star be twinned with *Tennyson*'s
A hundred years from now. So come, my friend,
   As soon as possible; come next weekend,
When Harry's children will be up with him –
   Who love you, James, as much as you love them.

– J. W. Barrs to James Thomson, 28 March 1882

*

Sir,

You will appreciate that your presence is no longer to be tolerated in this house. Since your own scotched apparatus will be unable to reconstruct the events of the early hours of this morning, may I record:
i) that earlier in your stay Miss Barrs had discovered flasks of what we take to be brandy concealed in the outbuildings – ii) that you went out with your pipe after supper and – despite our search and shouted entreaties – did not return at least until after we retired – which was as late as midnight – iii) your worse than nauseous condition – *before the children* – when you eventually unlocked your door this morning –
– which, taken together, prove your vow broken, and our trust betrayed – with what dreadful consequences.

As you pertly said before you disappeared, you cannot, with your means, hope to make recompense for the loss of 200 fowl, or for the damage the fire has done to the brooder house. Neither is it meaningful to 'thank' us for past kindnesses, as if these were likely to be repeated. I cannot wish you ill, only that you were better. But I despair of you.

– J. W. Barrs, draft letter, undated (?spring 1882); not sent

*

Nowhere is the verse feeble . . . the majesty of the line has always its full colouring, and marches under a banner. And you accomplish this effect with the utmost sobriety, with absolute self-mastery.
— George Meredith, letter to James Thomson, 27 April 1880

No news — except that he was still on the warpath and in very full paint.
— H. Hood Barrs to J. W. Barrs, 17 April 1882

Dear Mr Barrs,

Was I tipsy myself, would you say, when I promised
To track down your favourite Arsonist? Still, I was hot on the scent;
For I followed that soiled scrap of address to a Pimlico roomhouse
In the shade of a railbridge, spattered by pigeons — and rapped at the door
At nine in the morning on Monday — when I prayed he'd be *fit*, if I found him.

The landlord is Gibson, an irascible type with an air of long suffering,
Who, as I pronounced the offending initials, stepped back with a snort, —
And then, with sarcastic good manners, conducted me through to the scullery,
Where *guess what* had happened — scorched walls, and the floor awash
With charred rags, and chairlegs, and offal and cabbage, all sodden and sooty.

It appears that at five this Gibson had woken with smoke
 in his nostrils
And stumbled downstairs, grabbing at buckets of slop
 as he went,
To discover a fairsized bonfire ablaze in the heart of his kitchen,
And our hero, impassively viewing the scene from the warmth
 of an armchair,
Offering never a word of excuse – only after a while,

And then, very often, shouting out 'Heebson! *Olé! Olé!*
Señor *Heeb*son! *Olé!*' – alluding, I learned, to a wild
But unshakeable fancy of his that the landlord was secretly *Spanish*.
(For reference – it seems said Spaniard had dared in the
 earlier evening
Engage with his crapulous lodger on matters of *rent* –
 hence this.)

So Gibson had chucked him out 'sharp', and was voluble
 now in relief,
Being rid of that 'stink', as he put it, for good – crowing, indeed,
That if ever B— should darken his doorstep
 again, by G—,
He could count on a merry reception, etc. I bid him good day
And was happy for that to remain the extent of our new
 acquaintance . . .

But I hadn't been back for an hour, when Gibson came knocking
 at *mine* –
For listen – the whole of the time he'd been cursing the fellow
 to hell
B.V. had been upstairs asleep, in one of the unlet rooms!
Since G. in the heat of his temper had failed to recover
 the key –
Our Homer had simply slipped in while he fumed at his coffee
 and kippers!

This time, went meekly, it seems – though leaving his *mark*
    on the bed –
Remembering, he claimed, he'd business to see to, with 'friends
    in the park'
– Which G. took to mean with 'his brothers, them beasts what they
    keep behind bars'.
Since then, I report, no one's seen hide nor hair of him, –
    living or dead –
Including
            Yours Truly
                    (I wish I was sorry to say).

                    – Percy Holyoake to J. W. Barrs, 10 May 1882

                            *

'He's been taken very ill,' I urged. 'He can do no harm now. Won't
you take him in if we bring him?' The man emphasised his refusal
with an oath, and slammed the door.
                    – T. E. Clarke, account of events of 1 June 1882

With money, I believe I should never have a home, but be always
going to and fro the earth, and walking up and down in it.
            – James Thomson, in conversation, quoted in Leonard, p. 173

                            *

GENTLEMEN ARE REMINDED
THE READING ROOM IS NOT A HOSTEL
on barred doors, at midnight;
– and neither was I, the had-been
Arts-Clerk-in-Residence,
to dream of a bed in Reference.

Instead, to strip the carcass
of the Visiting Poets Scheme
I'd written up that morning:
LIVE HERE TONIGHT
THE AUTHOR OF 'INSOMNIA',
'THE WALKER', 'IN MY ROOM', ETC. –

The very man who now hogged the portal –
head first, as if to butt in five hours late
on his own abandoned reading,
but not so much as breathing
through the mask of custard, brandy, blood
his spatchcock nose had blurted.

Yet stooping as I did
to filch what work-in-progress
had stopped in those pockets,
the eyes in the back of my head
detected a less dead
statue hard by:

a stray from the museum,
but on its brow a crown
of fresh leaves shivered, and pulses
rippled the grooves of gown;
and when its finger moved to fix
the wet clay I straightened from

a stone voice ground out at me
(in English, with a marble accent),
'Relieve yourself at once on this head's flesh
The quicker to melt it into mulch and aether'
(so anxious to obey, I looked to find
I was already doing as he instructed) –

'For a reputation spoils in the library loft
With fox marks on the pages, and this
Oaf's glandular grin for a frontispiece:
This northern appetite – this *bon viveur* –
This bear-faced bevvying barbarian barnacle –
'B.V.', as he would have me style my poems.

An umpteenth birthday passed in a cage of rain;
Those small perennial hopes, for a collie and heather
And Harriet Barrs, as ash in the grate again:
That when he knocked and wheedled and begged and beavered
And roared to have our head, my self was spent,
And he dissolved us in his element.

But leave that – since the terms of my new estate
Are to walk as I have never walked before!'
So we did walk: he streets ahead, composing
a queer Senecan hopscotch, or drifting
beside me in companionable silence;
until the dark began to fade.

Then he pulled up, as if short of breath,
and seemed to be sweating, and needed a shave,
and offered his empty hand in a hurry:
'I leave the card of *The Rambler* magazine,
as I cannot be sure of my present address
for some time to come –' and was nothing

*Note: The estate of James Thomson – now a condemned housing scheme in
Greenock, Strathclyde – wishes to dissociate itself from the above.*

And some there be, which have no memorial, who are perished as
though they had never bene.
— Ecclesiasticus, 44 (Authorized Version, 1611)

But Galileo, in his notebook, the same year:
I saw the Milky Way — so long dismissed, and lightly,
as gases, raised to reflect the glow of the stars in their houses —
tonight, teem with its own rebellious armies of starlife;
and not for Earth's amusement — except through glasses, darkly —
our Zodiac being a false vault in the bowels of a Babel,
whose brightest lights, in the vast upstairs, will disappear. . . .

A free-for-all; vandals have knocked through the wonderful ceiling
and pitched Michelangelo down on the midden with Castor and Pollux;
and the notes of the scale are heard no more, or lanterns seen
than the holes between: or the wide estates between holes,
where heaven's unlikely guest revolves at his massive leisure
or bores his way through sleeps of aether; where the worst,
    fractious
asteroid beams in the thousand miles of her cold dominion.

And fair play to rejects — to busts with broken noses —
whose last great work was finding a shed or stable to die in,
if they dream away their loss of face in a sky like that;
if there, though the day's glare or northern night obscure them,
though nature has done with them, still through the void they
    hurtle their wattage,
powered with the purpose of having been — being, after all,
    stars,
whose measure we may not take, *nor know the wealth of their rays.*

Peter Reading

Fiction

Donald is a fictitious character
arrived at an age and bodily state
rendering suicide superfluous,
would rather sip Grands Crus than throw his leg.
He is a writer of fiction. He says
'Even one's self is wholly fictitious'.
Hatred once drew him to satiric verse
but he could think of nothing to rhyme with
'Manageress of the Angel Hotel',
or 'I call my doctor *"Killer" Coldwill*'
(a fictitious name, 'Coldwill', by the way),
or 'Headmaster of the Secondary Mod.'

Donald has created a character
called 'Donald' or 'Don' who keeps a notebook
dubbed 'Donald's Spleneticisms', e.g.:
'Complacent as a Country Town GP',
'Contemptible as County Council Clerks',
'A hateful little Welshman shared my train
with no lobes to his ears and yellow socks',
'Seedy as Salesmen of Secondhand Cars'.

In Donald's novel, 'Don' writes poetry –
titles such as 'It's a Small World', 'Fiction',
'Y – X', 'Remaindered', which he sends
to literary periodicals
under the nom de plume *'Peter Reading'*
(the present writer is seeking advice
from his attorney, Donald & Donald).
This fictitious bard has a doctor called
'Coldwill' who sleeps with the manageress
of the Angel (and sues 'Don' for libel).

In Donald's novel, 'Don' (whose nom de plume
is *'Peter Reading'*) sues a man whose *real*
name is 'Peter Reading' for having once
written a fiction about a poet
who wrote verse concerning a novelist
called 'Donald' whose book 'Fiction' deals with 'Don'
(a poet who writes satirical verse
and is sued by an incompetent quack,
the manageress of a pub, a Celt
with lobeless ears and yellow socks, acned
Council clerks and a Range Rover salesman).

In 'Reading's' fiction, the poet who writes
verse concerning the novelist 'Donald'
is sued by the latter who takes offence
at the lines '. . . an age and bodily state
rendering suicide superfluous,
would rather sip Grands Crus than throw his leg'.
For the Defence, 'Donald, QC' says that
'Even one's self is wholly fictitious'.

I am an abrasive wit,
an oasis of intellect.

Of my kind –
and there are not many of my kind –
I am really quite remarkably good.

I am mordant, very mordant.
Satire is clearly one of my gifts.

Out of everyday matters
I fashion urbane jokes.

My evocation of a seedy hotel room
is particularly liked.

Most of me is marked
by a bitter sense of humour.

I am reminiscent of
intellectual paper-games.

I can handle the Long Poem.

I contain some clever rhymes –
e.g. candid/Gran did.

I am a master of the narrative.
I am a master of the descriptive.

I am looked forward to
being heard from in the future.

ON THE OTHER HAND

I do not transcend pain with Poetry.

I am not as mellifluous as Sir John Betjeman.

I am not as good as
a very great number of people
(who do the same thing better).

Not all of me makes you laugh aloud
on the number 17 bus.

I am drab rhythmless demotic.

I am all very amusing in my way, maybe,
(and definitely mordant)
but am I Art?

?

Sired by *Surgical   Sundries Inc.*,
my appearance – patent   pending – is awesome.
I am not fettled from   fleeces of thick wool,
no knitter's needles   knocked me up.
Silkworms that dextrously   adorn the sleek web
with *wyrda cræftum*   couldn't make me;
yet, in institutions,   internationally
men will attest me   a tight-fitting raiment.

Say, supple-minded   master of wit,
wealthy in words,   what my name is.

Hardfhip Aboard American Sloop The Peggy, 1765

Sailed for New York from Azores,
October 24th,
American floop the *Peggy*
(Mafter, Captain Harrifon),
cargo of wine and brandy
alfo a negro flave.

Storm blew up from North-Eaft,
rigging feverely damaged,
could make no way, d'ye fee?
Harrifon rationed all hands,
one pound of dry bread per day,
one pint of water and wine.

Hull fprung breach below water,
two veffels paffed – foul conditions
prevented communications,
rations reduced by degrees,
no food or water remained,
hands drunk on brandy and wine.

By December 25th
clement weather prevailed,
a fail was fpied, but its fkipper,
damn his eyes, ignored our fignal,
all hands pierced the air with fcreams
more pitiful than mews' wails.

Only liveſtock aboard –
two pigeons and the fhip's cat,
doves flain for Chriſtmas Dinner,
flew the cat two days later,
divided it into nine,
head was the Captain's portion.

After the cat, the negro.
Fell on his knees, begged mercy.
Dragged him into the fteerage,
fhot through the head by James Doud.
Kindled a fire abaft
to fry entrails and liver.

Mr James Campbell, half ftarved,
rufhed forward, ripped out the liver,
ftuffed it raw into his mouth.
The reft of us, after feafting,
pickled the body's remains –
threw head and fingers o'erboard.

James Campbell died raving mad
three days later, from eating
the liver raw. Fearing much,
left we all contract his madnefs,
refrained from eating Campbell,
caft body unto the fea.

By January 26th
the corpfe of the flave was ate.
Drew lots to fee who was next,
myfelf, David Flat, foremaft man,
felected the fhorteft ftraw,
afked to be defpatched quickly.

Reft of the hands decided
to wait till 11 o'clock
next day before flaying me
left deliverance fhould arrive.
That night my fenfes quit me –
'tis faid they have not returned.

At 10 a veffel hove-to,
the *Sufannah* bound for London
(Mafter, Thomas Evers),
took furvivors aboard,
myfelf in a fwoon, raving,
reached Land's End March 2nd.

To this day fometimes I fee them:
Captain David Harrifon,
James Doud, Lemuel Afhley,
James Warren, Samuel Wentworth,
eyes like a frightened horfe's
of the neger, whites uplifted.

Tom o' Bedlam's Beauties*

In the summer hols we cycled
as far as the green water-tower
in the grounds of which grew apples.

Broken Bass bottles, embedded
in the cement-skimmed wall,
we bridged with tough hide school satchels.

Once within, we filched unripe
fruit – English old-fashioned names
like *Tom o' Bedlam's Beauties*.

The water-tower watchman, too,
had old-fashioned lingo – 'Grrr!
Young varmints!' – as in the *Beano*.

Returning, we munched apples under
another red brick buttressed wall.
Sated, we sought diversion.

Scaling a steep brick triangle,
peering over the parapet,
a prison-like scene was presented.

Close-cropped men in brown denim
tended a formal flower garden
behind which, a house with barred windows.

The nearest gardener glopped
but seemed not to see us, holding
his rake upside-down by the prongs.

*Old Herefordshire name for variety of eating-apple.

Another solemnly knelt
chewing the bloom of a red
Hybrid Tea – *Ena Harkness*, I think.

We pelted them with our cores
and all we could not consume.
Some of us scored direct hits.

The one with the upside-down rake
raised his palms to the sky
and visibly, audibly, wept.

Gigglingly biking back,
we resolved to repeat the prank
discreetly dubbed *Sanes and Loonies*.

Wandering

Permit me to parley – Brigadier Peregrine
Fashpoint-Shellingem (author of *Peruvian
Jungle by Kayak*, *With a Kodak in Kooju*,
Huskies Away!, *Hottentots Were My Neighbours*,
In the Bush with the Blacks of Booloo-Kishooloo,
&c. &c. &c. &c.),
KCB, MVO, FRGS.

                              Oh, I
know that I probably don't seem the type, as we
prune back this gnarled Hybrid Tea *Ena Harkness* and
rake the first leaves from the lawns to the compost heaps
tucked in triangular shadows of buttresses
(daily, the sun getting lower, the wall higher),
but, I assure you, the world *was* my whatsaname
(damn funny thing; can't remember the word for it).

Camped with the Indians, pure Tehuelche blood,
on the bleak plateaux of cold Patagonia,
cattle crashed down under bowled bolladores there –
feet drawn together noosed, tail stuck up rigidly.

Saw summers on the Salween when the river rose
fifty feet overnight flinging up cottage-sized
boulders like pitched pebbles, porters splashed into pulp.

Camped at the edge of the East Rongbuk Glacier,
gale reached its maximum, 1 a.m. 26th,
wild flapping canvas made noise like machine-gun fire,
fine frozen spindrift thrashed into our sleeping-bags.
Jettisoning empty oxygen-cylinders,
each clanged like church-bell rings into the East Rongbuk.

Fell through the floes with a dog-team in Labrador,
slashed free the harnesses, swam for the nearest ice,
stripped off my garments and beat the freeze out of 'em,
still couldn't last the night, had to kill all the dogs,
skinned 'em and made a rough coat with the hair inside,
piled up the dead bodies, cuddled up close to 'em,
lasted till morning, relief-ship arrived, by Gad.

Plied down the Pyrene River in wild Peru,
Indian, Quinchori, built twenty rafts for us,
bartered with five rolls of cloth, knives and ornaments,
balsa logs pinned with hard splinters of chonta wood,
spray flew on all sides up, rainbowing rays of sun . . .

Sometimes it seems a long, long while ago to me . . .
all I can do to remember events when that
damnation Matron, whatever her name is, says
'Now then, of *course* you're a brave, brave explorer man.
Tell Doctor' (whatsisname) 'Snyderson all about
nice Patagonia, "*Brigadier*" Peregrine.'

Phrenfy

The Mafter's phrenfy having continued long,
his left eye fwelled unto an hen's egg fize
fo that the furgeon daily feared 'twould burft.

Th' extreme pain of this tumour caufed the Mafter
to be awake a month. On fome occafion
it took four other perfons and myfelf
to hold him in reftraint 'gainft his defire
to tear his own eye out with his own hands.

Thence he continued filent one whole year.
In this ftate of poor helplefs idiocy
he languifhed.

        On November 30th
I went into his chamber – 'twas his birthday,
and bonfires and illuminations marked
th' refpect the townffolk felt at the event.
I fpoke to him about thefe preparations
to which he faid 'All folly, Mrs Ridgeway.
They had done better letting it alone.'

A few months afterwards, on my removing
a fharp knife from his grafp, he faid 'I am
that which I am, I am that which I am'
and in fix minutes, poor fad fimpleton,
whifpered the fame thing two or three times more.

One day, calling his fervant to his fide
but being quite unable to exprefs
any defires, he fhewed figns of diftrefs
and great uneafinefs and faid at length
'I am a fool'. On fome occafion later,
his fervant having taken away his watch,
he called the menial and faid 'Bring it here'.

His laft words, fpoken to his fervant when
that gentleman was breaking a large hard coal,
were, 'That is a ftone, you blockhead'. He was quiet
a twelvemonth afterwards and died in filence.

At Marsden Bay

Arid hot desert stretched here in the early
Permian Period – sand dune fossils
are pressed to a brownish bottom stratum.
A tropical saline ocean next silted
calcium and magnesium carbonates
over this bed, forming rough Magnesian
Limestone cliffs on the ledges of which
Rissa tridactyla colonizes –
an estimated four thousand pairs
that shuttle like close-packed tracer bullets
against dark sky between nests and North Sea.
The call is a shrill 'kit-e-wayke, kit-e-wayke',
also a low 'uk-uk-uk' and a plaintive
'ee-e-e-eeh, ee-e-e-eeh'.

Four boys about sixteen years old appear
in Army Stores combat-jackets, one wearing
a Balaclava with long narrow eye-slit
(such as a rapist might find advantageous),
bleached denims rolled up to mid-calf, tall laced boots
with bright polished toe-caps, pates cropped to stubble.
Three of the four are cross-eyed, all are acned.
Communication consists of bellowing
simian ululations between
each other at only a few inches range:
'Gibbo, gerrofforal getcher yaffuga',
also a low 'lookadembastabirdsmon'.

Gibbo grubs up a Magnesian Limestone
chunk and assails the ledges at random,
biffing an incubating kittiwake
full in the sternum – an audible slap.

Wings bent the wrong way, it thumps at the cliff base,
twitching, half closing an eye. Gibbo seizes
a black webbed foot and swings the lump joyously
round and round his head. It emits
a strange wheezing noise. Gibbo's pustular pal
is smacked in the face by the flung poultry, yowls,
and lobs it out into the foam. The four
gambol euphoric like drunk chimps through rock pools.
Nests are dislodged, brown-blotched shells crepitate
exuding thick rich orange embryo goo
under a hail of hurled fossilized desert
two hundred and eighty million years old.

Editorial

Being both *Uncle Chummy's Letter Box*
of *Kiddies' Column* and *Supa Scoop* besides
(*Your Headlines As They Happen*), and having the shakes
uncellophaning fags this crapulous morning,
I compose: BOY (13) CLUBS DAD TO DEATH,
CHILD (10) SCALDS GRANNY (87) TO DEATH,
SKINHEAD (14) STONES KITTIWAKES TO DEATH
AS RSPCA ASKS 'WHERE'S THE SENSE?'

Better this afternoon after the Vaults,
I award 50 pence to Adam (9)
for this: 'Dear Uncle Chummy, I am writing
to let you know about my hamster Charlie
who's my best friend . . .' 'Keep up the good work,
   kiddies . . .'
(sinister dwarfs, next issue's parricides).

P.S.

The stitching new on your tiny rectangle of black,
you immerse yourself in the sad therapy of the kitchen,
withdrawing from sight when assailed by trembling and
    weeping.
I mailed you my useless sympathy but, reticently,
withheld admiration and love for you (old-fashioned words)
who, having a grim chore to finish, get on with the job.

Hints

Find ways to make the narrative compel,
I advise students; as, in retailing this,
you might lend the issue added poignancy
by being distanced – describe the electrified
overgrown line in cool botanical terms,
white cow-parsley, *Anthriscus sylvestris*,
adding the child with anthropological
detachment, ten years old, print dress, bewildered . . .

Compelling, maybe, but mere narrative –
no moral or intellectual envoy.
Accentuate the dignified resilience
that humans, or some, are capable of still,
evinced in the sad braveness of the bereaved
whose daughter, being blind, observed no warning.

15th February

I tried to put in what I really felt.
I really tried to put in what I felt.
I really felt it – what I tried to put.
I put it really feelingly, or tried.
I felt I really tried to put it in.
What I put in I tried to really feel.
Really I felt I'd tried to put it in.
I really tried to feel what I put in.

It cost £5 in WH Smith's.
£5 it cost – WH Smith's ain't cheap.
£5 ain't cheap, not for a thing like that.
It costs, a thing like that – £5 ain't cheap.
It wasn't a cheap thing – £5 it cost.
A thing like that ain't cheap in WH Smith's.
In WH Smith's a thing like that comes costly.
A lot to pay, £5, for a thing like that.

The heart was scarlet satin, sort of stuffed.
I sort of felt it was me own heart, like.
SHE TORE THE STUFFING OUT OF THE SCARLET HEART.
I sort of stuffed and tore her sort of scarlet.
I stuffed her, like, and felt her sort of satin.
I sort of felt she'd tore out all me stuffing.
I felt her stuff like satin sort of scarlet
her stuff felt sore, torn satin whorlet scar
I liked her score felt stiffed her scar lick hurt
I tore her satin felt her stuffed her scarlet
tore out her heart stuff scarred her Satan har
I licked her stiff tore scarf her harlot hair

tied scarf tore stabbed scar whore sin sat tit star
stuffed finger scar ha ha ha ha ha ha
felt stiff scarf tight tore scarlet heart her scare
her scare stare stabbed heart scarlet feel torn mur

Found

Strange find – a plastic dummy from a boutique
(boots, white long thighs, pants pulled right down, a sack
over the head and torso) dumped among bins
and tumps of fetid garbage and coils of rank
sloppy dog faeces in an ill-lit alley
between the Launderette and Indian Grocer.
Incorrect diagnosis: it emits
a high-pitched rattle like Callas gargling.

Rescrutinizing 36 hours later:
what was, in sodium light, viridian,
is, in pale February sun, maroon.
About a soup-cupful remains still viscous,
black at the rim where a scabbed mongrel sniffs,
ripples taut sinew, salivates and laps.

Epithalamium

I

. . . have great pleasure in . . .
of their daughter Crystal . . .
enclosed Gift List . . .

    Dragonstraw door mat in plaited seagrass
from China.
    'Tik Tok' wall clock, battery operated
quartz movement in pine frame.
    'La Primula Stripe' dishwasher-proof
glazed earthenware coffee set.
    Valance with neat box pleats to fit
3ft to 5ft beds (fixed by Velcro pads).
    Michel Guérard's kitchen work table
with base of solid pine, including
a duckboard shelf for storage,
a knife rack and pegs for teacloths.
    Boxwood pastry crimper.
    'Confucius' 50% polyester,
50% cotton duvet cover.
    Pine wine rack.
    Pine lavatory paper holder.
    Solid pine toilet seat with chrome fittings
(coated with 6 layers of polyurethane).
    Iron omelette pan with curved sides.
    Angus Broiler cast iron pan for steaks
and chops which combines the ease of frying
with the goodness of grilling.
    'Leonardo' sofa in cream herringbone.
    Honey-coloured beech bentwood rocker
with cane back and seat.
    Cork ice-bucket with aluminium insert.
    'Mr Toad' rattan chair from France.
    Tough cotton canvas Sagbag filled
with flame-retardant polystyrene granules.

2

The fizz is Spanish, labelled MEGOD CHAMPAIN.

3

. . . have great pleasure in . . .
will now read Greetings Cards . . .

> de da de da de da de da this wedding gift to you
> de da de da de da de da your golden years come true . . .
> All the way from America . . .
> sorry can't be there . . .
> would love to have been there . . .
> a California 'Howdy!' . . .
> de da de da de da de da all your hopes and fears
> de da de da de da de da throughout the coming years . . .
> have made their bed, must *lay* in it . . .

HA HA HA HA HA HA HA (what a riot the Best Man *is*).

4

At their new home – 'Crimmond' (next to 'Sinatra' on one
    side
and 'Mon Rêve' on the other) – the presents are laid out.
They look lovely, don't they, Confucius, Leonardo and Mr
    Toad.

5

Bog paper and boots are tied to their bumper.
Consummation in Calais is nothing to write home about.

Carte Postale

Dear Mum and Dad,
                          The picture shows a 'gendarme'
which means policeman. France is overrated.
For two weeks it has been wet. 9th September:
we had a 'dégustation' in the Côte
de Mâconnais and Mal got quite light-headed.
Sometimes I think it will be *too* ideal
living with Mal – it's certainly the Real
Thing. I must go now – here comes Mal.
                                    Love, Crystal.

Encircling her slim waist with a fond arm,
the husband of a fortnight nibbles her throat,
would be dismayed to learn how she had hated
that first night when in Calais he had kissed all
over her, and, oh God!, how she now dreaded
each night the importunate mauve-capped swollen
    member.

from **Going On**

Sí señor, sure we har claiming the
bomb as Glorious Blow by
    Forces of Liberate Dark
    Dictate Oppression. Too long

far have we, fathers and hrandfathers
forced to Slavery lifes hwich
    Army of Liberate fight
    struggles till all mens are dead!

Down with the generalísimo!
(not the present or last hwon,
    only the hwon pefore last),
    Viva la Muerte! señor,

Viva el excelentísimo
Señor conde de Torre-
    gamberro! Yes sirs my friend,
    what is the matter that some

dies for the Cause of the hwons that is
thinking right in this matters?
    This she's Political's War.
    Sure what are some person lifes?

We not Guerrillas amigo but
Counter-Anti-Guerrilla
    them was our Leaders but now —
    those is our Enemy, sí,

ow you say por favor now they has
showed False Ideologics.
    Terrorist Actions too bad;
    this why we take such Campaigns!

This very Positive Actions she
may have kill some who have no
    doings with Rebels but so?
    Bombs she not go off for fun.

Don't say amigo you not with the
understandings of why we
    fights in montañas of South?
    This are the struggles to death!

OK so 20 am dead and some
shrapnels goes to some peoples –
    we har of People's own blood!
    This is of why we shall fight!

Last bomb was not our bomb *that* was bomb
blown hwen Traitor who carries
    gets it hexplosure too soon
    killing himself and some mans.

Somehow you get mix up, señor, you
see we Neutral in all thing
    this hwy the reasons hwe fights!
    Freedoms to Govermans Farce!

Same Costa Rica but also with
Nicaraguan Border!
    Now you mus hunderstand well
    which why this bombs must hexplode.

                    *

'Outraged of Telford' has written to
tell the Editor how, last
    Saturday, she and her spouse
    went to the Precinct to shop.

There was 'a group of young teenagers
lounging round in a doorway',
    spawling and picking their spots.
    One, a girl aged about 12,

moved from her mates to the side of the
old chap (husband of 'Outraged'),
    where she took hold of his arm,
    disgorged her pink bubble-gum,

said to him 'What do you think of the
youth of Telford, eh, sexy?'
    'Not very much', he replied,
    shaking her free of his arm.

Whereupon she became violent,
spat phlegm into the man's face,
    screamed 'Well I'll tell you what, cunt,
    we think *you're* old fucking shits!'

('Outraged of Telford' has written it
c dash t, for discretion;
    similarly f dash g;
    similarly s dash t.)

[As I have elsewhere remarked, these are
times which baffle the oldies –
    wee kiddiwinkies infest,
    parricide, parricide soon . . .]

                    *

These are the days of the horrible headlines,
BOMB BLAST ATROCITY, LEAK FROM REACTOR,
SOCCER FANS RUN AMOK, MIDDLE EAST BLOOD BATH,
PC KNOCKS PRISONER'S EYE OUT IN CHARGE ROOM.
Outside, the newsvendors ululate. Inside,
lovers seek refuge in succulent plump flesh,

booze themselves innocent of the whole shit-works.
Why has the gentleman fallen face-forward
into his buttered asparagus, Garçon?
He and his girlfriend have already drunk two
bottles of Bollinger and they were half tight
when they arrived at the place half an hour since.
Waiters man-handle the gentleman upright,
aim him (with smirks at the lady) towards his
quails (which he misses and slumps in the gravy –
baying, the while, for 'Encore du Savigny').
He is supplied with the Beaune, which he noses,
quaffs deeply, relishes . . . sinks to the gingham
where he reposes susurrantly. There is
'63 Sandeman fetched to revive him.
Chin on the Pont l'Évêque, elbow in ash-tray,
as from the *Book of the Dead*, he produces
incomprehensible hieroglyphs, bidding
Access surrender the price of his coma
unto the restaurateur, kindly and patient.
These are the days of the NATIONAL HEALTH CUTS,
days of the end of the innocent liver;
they have to pay for it privately, who would seek anaesthetic.

*

This is unclean: to eat turbots on Tuesdays,
tying the turban unclockwise at cockcrow,
cutting the beard in a south-facing mirror,
wearing the mitre whilst sipping the Bovril,
chawing the pig and the hen and the ox-tail,
kissing of crosses with peckers erected,
pinching of bottoms (except in a yashmak),
flapping of cocks at the star-spangled-banner,
snatching the claret-pot off of the vicar,
munching the wafer without genuflexion,
facing the East with the arse pointing backwards,

thinking of something a little bit risqué,
raising the cassock to show off the Y-fronts,
holding a Homburg without proper licence,
chewing the cud with another man's cattle,
groping the ladies – or gentry – o'Sundays,
leaving the tip on the old-plum-tree-shaker,
speaking in physics instead of the Claptrap,
failing to pay due obeisance to monkeys,
loving the platypus more than the True Duck,
death without Afterlife, smirking in Mecca,
laughing at funny hats, holding the tenet
how that the Word be but fucking baloney,
failing to laud the Accipiter which Our Lord saith is Wisdom.

Started by *Australophithecus*, these are
time-honoured Creeds (and all unHoly doubters
shall be enlightened by Pious Devices:
mayhems of tinytots, low-flying hardwares,
kneecappings, letterbombs, deaths of the firstborns,
total extinctions of infidel unclean wrong-godded others).

*

There is a reciprocity here of maniac malice.
Theists are butchers, and twerpish their god-loves,
vicious PC punches prisoner's eye out,
Angels euphorically slaughter their buddies,
some PMs have Special Men to do-in your
Mrs or nipper or you if you vote wrong,
kiddies are calling us cunts and will kill us,
addle-brained Counter-revs. maim all and sundry,
man sets to work on his neighbour with rip-saw,
horrified mum watches mugger stab tot blind,
niggers are here to be murdered in season,
OAP women are here to be fucked with lavatory brushes,
my little baby annoys me – I burn it, punch off the blisters.

[Bit of a habit, the feigned indignation,
various metres, Alcmanics and so forth,
ludic responses to global débâcles.
   Just Going On remains possible through the
slick prestidigital art of Not Caring/Hopelessly Caring.]

*

Reps and execs in *Plastics* and *Packaging*
(holiday-wise it's Costa del Parvenu),
   Fitments and *Fords*, complete Expenses
      Forms for their Beer'n'Byte basket scampi.

They are disgusting; I am a secular
saint of the breed Empiricist Atheist
   (here is a quid for Oxfam hapless
      starving in sewer-pipes somewhere beastly).

*

Media elbow-deep in the offal-bin
(FLENSED-ALIVE MPS MANGLED IN BOMB-ATTACK),
   nincompoop zealots toy with jelly,
      Crass Kakistocracies viva, viva . . .

from **Perduta Gente**

South Bank: Sibelius 5's
incontrovertible end –
five exhalations, bray of expiry,
     absolute silence . . .

Under the Festival Hall is a foetid
     tenebrous concert
  strobed by blue ambulance light.
  PVC/newspapers/rags
insulate ranks of expendables, eyesores,
     winos, unworthies,
one of which (stiff in its cardboard Electrolux
     box stencilled FRAGILE,
  STOW THIS WAY UP, USE NO HOOKS)
  officers lug to the tumbril,
  exhaling, like ostlers, its scents:

              squit,

              honk,

              piss,

              meths,

              distress.

*

One day a lone hag gippo arrived and
     camped on the waste ground
which we traversed on our way to the school bus
     every morning.

Cumulus breath puffs rose from a pink-nosed
      rope-tethered skewbald.
Winter: a frost fern fronded the iced glass
      caravan window
through which I ventured a peep, but I leapt back
      horribly startled
  when the rime cleared and an eye
  glared through the hole at my own.
(Filthy she was, matted hair, withered leg and
      stank of excreta.)

After that, each time we passed it we'd lob a
      rock at the window.
When it was smashed she replaced it with cardboard;
      one of us lit it –
she hobbled round with a pisspot and doused the
      flames with its contents.
Then she gave up and just left it a gaping
      black fenestration
  through which we chucked bits of scrap,
  rubbish, a dog turd, a brick.

  But when she skedaddled, a stain,
  delineating where she'd been,
  etiolated and crushed,
  blighted that place, and remained.

*

Now we arrive at the front of the ruin;
      here are there moanings,
shrieks, lamentations and dole,
here is there naught that illumes.
Mucky Preece lives in a pigsty beside the
      derelict L Barn,
  tetrous, pediculous, skint,
  swilling rough cider and Blue.

Now lie we sullenly here in the black mire —
        this hymn they gurgle,
    being unable to speak.
    Here they blaspheme Divine Power.
MONEY NO OBJECT TO BUYER OF L-SHAPED
        PICTURESQUE OLD BARN
    SEEKING THE QUIET COUNTRY LIFE
    (two hundred and twenty-two grand,
    Property Pages last night —
    with which Mucky Preece is involved,
    scraping the squit from his arse).

                    *

Snarl of a JCB, cordon of Old Bill,
        megaphone rasping
    into a 3 a.m. squat.

Sleep-fuddled dissolutes, still dressing cold dis-
        consolate bratlings,
    struggle with carrier-bags.

One of the Council Bailiffs is sporting a
        HAVE A NICE DAY badge
    fixed on the yellow hard hat.

                    *

Often at dusk in the birch woods beyond the
        gates of the city,
you see the glimmer of fires of the hapless
        dispossessed losers.

One of these, russetly lit from beneath by
        fulminant embers,
    howls through the tenebrous gloom —
    something concerning smoked fish,
    black bread and vodka, I think.

Distant, a plangently-played balalaika ac-
        companies wailing
    vocals whose burden is loss –
Gone are the youthfully beautiful whom I
        loved in my nonage;
    strength and vitality, gone;
    roof-tree and cooking-hearth, gone.

Eyes like an elephant's, blood-bleared and tiny,
        gowkily ogle;
tremulous wart-knuckled pachyderm fingers
        fumble a tin cup;
skewers of carp flesh fumed to mahogany;
        dark-crusted rye loaf;
    sloshed spirit hissing in ash.

                    *

    Don't think it couldn't be you –
    bankrupted, batty, bereft,
huddle of papers and rags in a cardboard
        spin-drier carton,
bottle-bank cocktails and Snow soporifics,
        meths analgesics,
beg-bucket rattler, no-hope no-homer,
        squatter in rat-pits,
    busker in underground bogs
    (plangent the harp-twang, the *Hwaet!*
Haggard, the youthful and handsome whom I
        loved in my nonage;
    vanished, the vigour I valued;
    roof-tree and cooking-hearth, sacked).
    Bankrupted, batty, bereft –
    don't think it couldn't be you.

                    *

That one is Boris the Swine
(known as 'the Swine' for the fact that he sometimes
        falls in the swine-pen
    when he is terribly drunk –
    covered in slurry for days),
but we must make allowances, since he
        worked at the Station
    when the – remember the headline
(EFFORTS ARE NOW BEING MADE TO ENCASE THE
        DAMAGED REACTOR)?

Often at evening he plangently strums and
        bays from the birch wood,
    where he reposes, this strain:
    Nothing can ever be done;
    things are intractably thus;
all know the bite of grief, all will be brought to
        destiny's issue;
those who have precognition suffer
        sorrow beforehand;
bodies are bankrupt, the main Expedition has
        left us behind it.

                    *

How doeth the citie sit solitarie that
        was full of people?
She that was great among nations hath no
        comforter, all her
    friends haue dealt treacherously.

Something is in the air, more and more nutters,
        alcos and dossers,
        dole diuturnal.

Sometimes it seems like a terrible dream from
        which we'll awaken;
   but mostly it seems that we won't.

Let us descend, though, through urinous subways to
        miseries greater,
al doloroso ospizio, where the
        newly tormented
        sample new torments.

   Woe vnto them that decree
   vnrighteous decrees and that turn
   the needy from iustice and robbe
   the rights from the poore of my people.

   What will ye doe with yr wealth
   in the day of the storme which shall come
   from afarre, when all that remaines
   is to crouch with those ye haue oppressed?

*

These who have never lived, blind lives so mean they
        envy all others,
   caitiffs whose deep-wailing plaints,
   horrible outcries, hoarse sighs,
Even in duff weather I'd rather do a
        skipper than stop there –
   trouble of kiphouses is
   vermin and no privacy.
piercing the starless air, dark-stained, dolent;
        when I remember,
   terror still bathes me in sweat –
   their thunderous outbreathing of woe.
Hundreds of beds and the blankets is never
        changed off the last one –
   crabs, you can pick up like that.

No fucking plugs in the sinks.
From the tormented Sad, sigh-troubled breath a-
rises around them,
crowds that are many and great,
children and women and men.
Bloke in the next bed to me (I could see him)
          pissed in his pillow
    then he just slep on it wet.
    Some on em masturbates, loud.
Let us not speak of them, merely observe and
silently pass by.

*

Outside Victoria Station a quorum of
          no-hoper foetid
impromptu imbibers is causing a shindy:
          one of the number,
clutching a bottle of Thunderbird, half full,
          rolls amongst litter
(chip-papers, Pepsi cans, Embassy packets –
          Indian take-out
    remnants adhere to her mac);
    under one arm is a crutch
    (the other is lopped at the elbow);
plaster encases her leg, which a colleague
          (sipping a Carlsberg)
kicks periodically, bellowing 'fugg-bag,
          fuggbagging fugg-bag'.

*

Newspaper, wrapped round the torso between the
          fourth and fifth jerseys
(night attire proper for doing a skipper in
          icy December
    under the Festival Hall),

carries a note to the Editor, from 'Ex-
        Soldier' of Telford,
    outlining plans to withdraw
    DHSS cash from those
    no-fixed-abode parasites.

Wound round a varicose indigo swollen
        leg, between second
    and third pair of trousers (which stink –
    urine and faeces and sick),
Property Pages delineate *bijou*
        River-View Flatlets
    £600,000 each.

*

[And don't think it couldn't be *you*:
grievously wounded veteran of the
        Battle of Bottle,
    jobless, bereft of home, skint,
down in the cold uriniferous subway
        spattered with drooled spawl,
lying in layers of newspaper ironies –
        Property Prices,
smug To the Editor platitudes on The
        Vagrancy Issue,
    ads for Gonzalez Byass;
dosser with Top Man carrier-bag, en-
        swathed in an *FT*;
Gizzera quiddora fiftyfer fuggsay,
        bankrupted, I been,
    fugginwell bankrupted, me;
    dolent, the wail from the Tube;
    and don't think it couldn't be *you*.]

*

Back of the Maximart, Saturday evenings:
        sometimes they chuck out
edibles (Sell By or Best Before dates of
        which have expired –
   Cheese 'n' Ham Tasties, Swiss Rolls,
   Ready-to-Microwave-Burgers)
   into a skip in the alley.
   Tonight it is minty ice-cream.

Icy December: three rank expendables
        squat on a split tomb
   covered in carroty spew,
one has his cock loose and pisses all over him-
        self and his colleagues –
   steam from both this and their breaths.
Each grasps a 2-litre polythene tub from
        which is extracted
scoopings of green ice by black half-mooned fingers.
        Slurping and beard-smirch,
   guzzle and emerald puke,
punctuate pulls from the communal Blue of
        methyl amnesia.

*

Legions of comatose owners of nothing
        under the concrete
   arches are juddered awake,
   impotent, dolent, bereft.

   Radioactive spent rods,
bound for reprocessing from the reactors,
        carried in finned flasks,
rumble by railway by night through a city
        hugely unconscious.

Nothing can ever be done;
  things are intractably thus;
knowing the bite of grief, all will be brought to
        destiny's issue;
those having precognition suffer
        sorrow beforehand.

Grief-bitten impotent owners of nothing,
        holding opinions
  gagged, disregarded, unsought.

*

Carrying on as though nothing is wrong is
        what we are good at:
  incontrovertible end;
  shrieks, lamentations and dole;
  lost livers, roof-trees and hearths;
on the waste ground at the back of the factory
        there's a crone scumbag
  that kips in a big cardboard box,
  etiolated and crushed;
those having precognition suffer
        madness beforehand
(EFFORTS ARE NOW BEING MADE TO ENCASE IN
        CONCRETE THE . . .); meanwhile,
here is a factory daily producing
        thousands of badges
  emblazoned with HAVE A NICE DAY.

Acknowledgements

The poems in this selection are taken from the following books, to whose publishers acknowledgement is made: *Tale of the Mayor's Son* (Bloodaxe, 1990), *Out of the Rain* (Bloodaxe, 1992), *Gnyss the Magnificent* (Chatto & Windus, 1993) and *Rest for the Wicked* (Bloodaxe, 1995) by Glyn Maxwell; *The Zoologist's Bath and Other Adventures* (Sycamore Press, 1982) and *Birthmarks* (Chatto & Windus, 1987) by Mick Imlah; *Fiction* (Secker & Warburg, 1979), *Tom o' Bedlam's Beauties* (Secker & Warburg, 1981), *Diplopic* (Secker & Warburg, 1983), *Going On* (Secker & Warburg, 1985) and *Perduta Gente* (Secker & Warburg, 1989) by Peter Reading.